More little BIG LEAGUERS™

By Bruce Nash and Allan Zullo
Compiled by Tom Muldoon

LITTLE SIMON
Published by Simon & Schuster
New York · London · Toronto · Sydney · Tokyo · Singapore

ACKNOWLEDGMENTS

We wish to thank all the players' parents, relatives, friends, and former coaches for generously helping us obtain childhood photographs. Among others who were kind enough to help in our photo search were Eris Northern, Ray Schulte, Bob Woods, Editor of *Topps Magazine*, and Sheila Young.

We are grateful to the following reporters who contributed valuable player interviews: Bill Althaus, Barry Bloom, Ron Cook, Bob Duff, Joe Giulotti, Larry LaRue, Carrie Muskat, Mike Paolercio, Tom Pedulla, Rob Rains, Barry Rozner, Larry Schwartz, Bill Shaikin, Larry Stone, and Casey Tefertiller.

We also appreciate the help we received from Julio Mateus, Sy Sussman, Kathy Zullo, and the public relations offices of the major league teams.

PHOTO CREDITS

Cover color photos by Tom DiPace.

Inside action photos by DiPace: Lee Guetterman, Don Mattingly, Jesse Barfield, Kelly Gruber, Bobby Thigpen, Tom Brunansky, Terry Pendleton, Lonnie Smith, Nick Esasky, and Vince Coleman. Andre Dawson photo by Stephen Green. All other inside action photos by the major league teams.

Little Simon
Simon & Schuster Building, Rockefeller Center
1230 Avenue of the Americas, New York, New York 10020

10 9 8 7 6 5 4 3 2 1

ISBN: 0-671-73394-X

★ ★ ★

To my Forest Hill High School classmates — the
Class of '65 — for your encouragement, interest,
and support. You always knew I could do it — even
before I did.

B.N.

To Jodi, Jill, Jeff, Audrae, Bess, Ray and Zeke —
with hopes that one day we'll all be playing
together on the same team.

A.Z.

For my dad, who thought baseball was the greatest
game ever invented and whose lifelong wish was
to see the Boston Red Sox crowned champions.
Through eternity, he'll occupy the best seat in
Fenway Park.

T.M.

After our first book in the *little BIG LEAGUERS*™ series was published, we discovered more funny, sad, zany, and inspiring childhood stories of major leaguers. So we decided to do *MORE little BIG LEAGUERS*™.

We interviewed super stars, All-Stars, rookies, and veterans about their days playing little league or sandlot baseball. When we approached the players, they were delighted to tell about their early days growing up on the baseball diamond. Some of the players revealed their amazing boyhood experiences for the very first time.

As kids, the players weren't all angels. Barry Larkin of the Cincinnati Reds admitted that he once deliberately got thrown out of a game because he didn't want to pitch. And the Atlanta Braves' Lonnie Smith confessed that he threw such a tantrum over an umpire's call that he stripped down to his underwear in the middle of the field in protest!

Crazy things have happened on the little league diamond. David Cone of the New York Mets recalled the game when his wild throw conked an umpire on the head and knocked him out. And Kansas City Royals star Kevin Seitzer remembered the time he was tagged out when he jumped up off the base in joy after hitting a clutch double.

Then there are the stories that are simply incredible. For two years in a row, the Cincinnati Reds' Bill Doran was one strike away from pitching his team to a Little League championship. But both times he gave up a disastrous game-winning home run—to the same batter! Will Clark of the San Francisco Giants was only $2\frac{1}{2}$ years old when his dog, Flash, twice came home with a left-handed first baseman's mitt in his mouth. Will used those gloves throughout his childhood and today is a super star left-handed first baseman.

In addition to the players themselves, their parents, former coaches, and teammates told their sides of the stories as well. They also helped us obtain photos of these stars as they looked in their little league glory days. These photos accompany the stories in this book, and they also appear on the baseball cards in the special bonus section at the back.

Perhaps when you read the book, you'll identify with some of the experiences—both good and bad—that these players had in their youth. Who knows? Perhaps one day *your* story will appear in a book about little leaguers who made it to the big leagues.

WILL CLARK

If it hadn't been for the family dog, Flash, Will Clark might never have become a first baseman.

"This is the greatest true dog story in history," declared Will's dad, Bill. "Flash really had an impact on Will's life in Little League."

When the San Francisco Giants' super star was 2½ years old, he lived in Petal, Mississippi, a tiny town of seven hundred people. He was too young to play baseball, so he spent his time throwing rocks and roughhousing in the yard with Flash, a black half-Labrador, half-pointer.

"We had no fence in our yard," recalled Will's dad. "In fact, most of the people in town didn't have fences. So Flash was free to roam the area. One day, he came home with a baseball glove in his mouth. It was a left-handed first baseman's mitt—used, but in good condition.

"We had no idea whose mitt it was. So we went to the one service station, the one drugstore, and the one grocery store in town and asked if anyone knew of a boy who was missing a glove. But no one claimed it."

Two weeks later, Flash trotted home again with another left-handed first baseman's mitt. Only this one was brand new. "We figured it had to belong to somebody who lived close by," recalled Bill. "We went all over the neighborhood, stopped every kid, and asked, 'Whose glove is this?' but no one knew." The Clarks even put an ad in the paper and tacked up a sign at the service station. When no one claimed either mitt, the Clarks decided to keep the gloves.

As fate would have it, Will was a left-hander. When he turned 7 and joined a baseball team for the first time, his parents gave him the old glove that Flash had found. "By the time he was 9 years old and on a Little League team, Will was playing first base," said his mother, Letty. "He was pretty good at it, too. Then, when Will was 12, we gave him the other glove—the new one. With that glove, Will got real good at picking up those short-hop throws from the infielders. He kept getting better and better at first base.

"Will really took care of those gloves. At the end of each season, he would oil the glove he had used and put it away. Then, a month before the baseball season, he'd break it in again by playing catch with his dad.

"It sure makes you wonder about Flash and those gloves, like maybe he knew something about Will's future that the rest of us didn't." What's so remarkable was that after Flash had brought home the two gloves, he never again stole another article of any kind.

Flash wasn't the only family dog that figured in Will's boyhood baseball life. When Will was 14 and living in New Orleans, he and his parents and his younger sister, Robin, would go to a nearby park where Will would hit batting practice. "My husband would pitch, and Robin and I would chase down the balls that Will would hit," recalled his mother. "Well, I got tired of this, so I went home and brought back our Labrador retriever, Shotsie, and stuck him out in center field. That dog ran all over the park and retrieved all the long balls that Will hit."

But it is Flash that the family remembers most. "Thanks to him, we didn't have to buy Will a glove until he was a senior in high school," said Bill. "Throughout his childhood, Will used only the gloves that Flash had found. I guess Will was destined to be a first baseman."

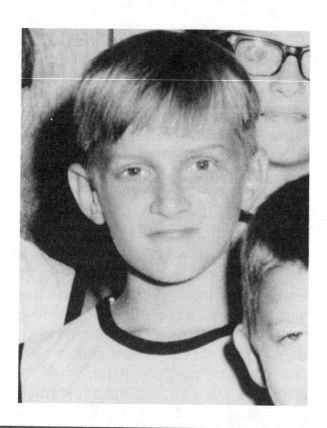

Third Baseman

Kansas City Royals

★ ★ ★

A funny thing happened to Kevin Seitzer on his way to hitting what appeared to be a game-tying home run. He made such a wide turn rounding third base that he ran into one of his own teammates. By the time Kevin got untangled, he was tagged out at the plate for the last out of the game.

"That sure was embarrassing," admitted the Kansas City Royals' star infielder. "I didn't know how to handle the situation. So I just broke down and cried."

Kevin's "homer that never was" happened when he was 9 years old and playing for the Middletown (Illinois) Little League team against its fiercest rival, New Holland.

In the bottom of the sixth inning, Kevin's team was losing 3-1 when he came to bat with two outs and a man on first. Kevin took a called strike and a ball before walloping the next pitch over the left fielder's head. Since there were no fences, the only way to get a homer was to run it out. Kevin's hit traveled so far, it looked like a sure game-tying home run.

"The runner on first scored easily and I came tearing around third base as the outfielder was just picking up the ball," Kevin recalled. "My dad was coaching third and waved me on. I knew I had a home run."

He was wrong. Kevin's teammates were wildly cheering him on from the bench, which was on the third base side of the field. They leaped off the bench and ran excitedly toward the third base line. Meanwhile, Kevin took an extra wide turn around third and headed for home. "Kevin ran smack into [teammate] David Becker," Kevin's dad, Cliff, recalled. "David was a big kid, and both he and Kevin fell down in a heap."

Kevin fought to untangle himself. He

finally got back up and started running toward home. But when he was about 10 feet from the plate, the ball came zipping into New Holland's catcher, and he tagged the diving Kevin for the final out of the game. What should have been an extra-inning game turned into a shocking 3-2 loss for Middletown.

"Everyone on our team had been hooting and hollering," Kevin recalled. "Now, there was dead silence. We'd lost . . . and I cried."

Kevin's dad, who was the team's coach, took the defeat calmly. He told Kevin that things like that happen in baseball. It was part of the game. However, Coach Seitzer did order his players to stay on the bench to avoid a similar incident in the future.

Five years later, when Kevin was 14 years old and playing on the Lincoln American Legion team, another dramatic last-inning hit turned into disaster. His team was down by one run in the ninth inning. There were two outs and a runner on second when Kevin smacked a double, driving in the tying run. A proud and happy Kevin slid into second, representing the winning run.

"Kevin was so happy about hitting the double that he began jumping up and down on second base," his dad recalled. "The outfielder threw the ball into the second baseman, who watched Kevin jump. Suddenly, as Kevin jumped straight up, the second baseman tagged him and the umpire called Kevin out."

Kevin was astonished. He didn't realize that when he jumped up, he was no longer on the bag and could be tagged out. "Kevin had the dumbest expression on his face," his dad recalled. "He couldn't believe he was out.

"Afterward, I reminded him of how getting excited had cost him a game when he was in Little League. I suggested he try to control his excitement the next time. It was costing us too many games."

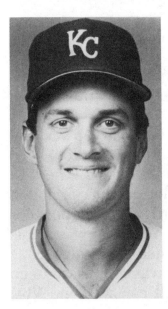

DARRYL STRAWBERRY

Outfielder
—
New York Mets

★ ★ ★

When Darryl Strawberry was a boy, he loved his baseball cap so much that he wore it from the time he got up in the morning until he went to sleep at night.

And sometimes he even wore it to bed.

The future New York Mets' All-Star slugger grew up in the poverty-stricken neighborhood of Watts in Los Angeles, where he played baseball with his two older brothers, Michael and Ronnie, in a nearby park. One day when Darryl was 8 years old, little league coach Obie Anderson watched the Strawberry brothers play and saw that they all had talent. He asked them to join his team, the Black Sox. They jumped at the chance. Darryl was now a member of a real team and was given his first official baseball cap.

He treasured that black cap. From the moment he first put it on his head, Darryl felt like a true baseball player. He was proud. And he wanted the world to know it, too.

"Darryl made that baseball cap a part of his head," his mom, Ruby, recalled. "You couldn't get him to take it off. The first thing he did in the morning was to put on his cap before he even left his bedroom. He wore it everywhere. When he was in his regular clothes, he had that cap on his head. Even when he wasn't dressed to go outside, that baseball cap was on. Why, there were times when he didn't even have to comb his hair because he wore that cap.

"Sometimes he'd come to the dinner table with his cap on. He knew he wasn't supposed to wear it, but he'd just forget that he had it on. I always had to tell him to take it off. He'd apologize and take off his cap, but he would put it under his leg so he was still touching it. The moment dinner was finished, the cap would go back on."

Darryl was not only a slugger on the Black Sox, he was also one of their best pitchers. When he wasn't playing in a league game or at practice, he was trying to get a sandlot game going. He just couldn't get enough baseball. "You'd see him in the neighborhood with his bat on his shoulder looking to play baseball," said his mother.

Ruby Strawberry loved watching her three sons play on the same team. But there was one problem. "All three boys were about the same size, so their caps were the same size, too," she said. "They constantly argued over whose cap was whose." When Michael and Ronnie tried to swipe Darryl's cap a few times, Darryl began taking it to bed with him at night and wearing it throughout the day.

After playing several seasons with the Black Sox, Darryl and his family moved into the Crenshaw district of West Los Angeles. And he soon stopped wearing his prized black cap.

It happened one day when he was playing catch with a friend who was on a little league team called the Padres. "I was pitching and the Padres' coach saw me," Darryl recalled. "He came right over and asked me my name and if I wanted to play baseball. I said sure."

Darryl was signed up on the spot and given a new wine-colored baseball cap, which he promptly put on his head. Said his mom, "He wouldn't take this cap off his head, either."

GREGG OLSON

Pitcher

Baltimore Orioles

★ ★ ★

Ten-year-old Gregg Olson was pitching in the biggest game of his life. It was for the championship of the Keystone Little League in Omaha, Nebraska.

But his control had deserted him. And to make matters worse, the opposing coach had ordered his batters not to swing at any of Gregg's pitches.

"I didn't understand what was going on, but I knew something wasn't right," recalled the Baltimore Orioles' All-Star reliever and 1989 Rookie of the Year. "The other players weren't even trying to swing. They just stood there with their bats on their shoulders until I walked them."

Gregg was taught to play hard but fair. That's why it didn't seem right to him that the other team wouldn't even try to hit his pitches, which were barely out of the strike zone. But the batters just stood at the plate until Gregg walked them—and then they laughed at him as they trotted down to first base.

Gregg was a good fast ball pitcher who seldom had control problems. In fact, almost every summer evening, he threw to his dad, Bill, in their backyard and learned to fire the ball into the strike zone nine out of ten times. So when he lost his control in the championship game, it happened at the worst possible time.

"It seemed like every year our Little League team wound up in second place," he said. "We either didn't score runs or we made too many dumb errors. I always went home a loser. Something always seemed to go wrong. So when I lost my control, I just thought, 'Here we go again!'"

His team was ahead 2-0 in the third inning when Gregg suddenly couldn't find the strike zone. The other team's coach immediately took advantage of the situation by ordering his players to leave their bats on their shoulders. "I filled the bases and then walked in four runs to put them ahead 4-2," Gregg recalled. "I was mad at myself for walking everyone. But I couldn't figure out why they wouldn't even attempt to swing at some of my pitches."

But Gregg's dad knew. He overheard the opposing coach order his batters not to swing. So Bill Olson marched up to the coach to complain. "I made it clear that this was not the intent of Little League baseball," Bill recalled. "The fun of baseball is swinging the bat whether you get a hit or not. The coach was taking that thrill away from the kids. And the true spirit of the game is to put your best hitting up against the other team's best pitching and see who comes out on top."

The coach listened to Gregg's dad and then changed his no-swing order. Gregg finally retired the side without giving up any more runs.

Gregg waited until the last inning to get his revenge. With his team still trailing 4-2, he came to bat with two runners on base. "I was never a good hitter," Gregg said. "In fact, until I got to high school, I was afraid of the ball. I used to duck out of the batter's box."

But not during this time at bat. Gregg dug in his heels and belted the first pitch. It sailed over the center fielder's head for a dramatic, game-winning, three-run home run! "I hung in there and hit a homer that won the game and the championship," said Gregg. "Boy, what a thrill that was!"

ANDRE DAWSON

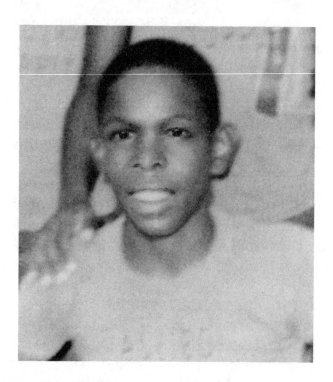

Andre Dawson was once scratched from the lineup after he protested the coach's choice of players for the starting team.

"It was my first and only suspension from baseball," recalled the Chicago Cubs' slugger and National League's Most Valuable Player in 1987. "I argued with the coach, who was my uncle and the head of the league. He made me sit down."

Andre's uncle, Curtis Taylor, was a student on summer break from classes at Florida A & M University in Tallahassee, Florida. Curtis realized that there was no baseball program for the boys in Andre's poverty-stricken neighborhood in Miami. So Curtis, who was spending the summer as an assistant recreation director at Lee Park, purchased bats and baseballs with his own money to use in a small league that he formed.

Andre was 9 years old when he and his neighborhood pals joined the league. He played for the Tigers, while his Uncle Curtis coached the Dodgers. At a game between the two teams, Andre's coach didn't show up on time. "Since the other coach wasn't there, I made up the Tigers' starting lineup," Curtis recalled. "Andre didn't like that."

Young Andre took one look at the lineup card and protested to Curtis. "I felt there was one boy starting who shouldn't start," Andre recalled. "I thought my uncle was trying to make sure that his team would win."

Curtis was outraged when Andre argued with him. So the coach suspended Andre on the spot. "He took me out of the starting lineup," Andre recalled. "He made me sit on the bench. I was crying about it. I wanted to go home and tell my grandmother, who was my uncle's mother, what he did."

Andre's suspension was brief. His own coach showed up after a couple of innings and inserted Andre into the lineup. Andre was still angry at Curtis, though, and when he went home, Andre complained to his grandmother. "She told me that I shouldn't argue with authorities," he recalled. "She said I should show some respect. I remember that to this day."

Curtis, who today is an assistant principal at Devon-Aire Elementary School in Miami, said, "It taught Andre a lesson. He shouldn't have been so quick to jump to conclusions that someone was trying to cheat him. In actuality, I didn't care who won the game as long as every boy there got to play. Andre later understood that, and he learned some sportsmanship from having to sit out the start of the game."

When the summer league ended, Andre continued to play all forms of baseball the year round. "Andre would throw rocks up in the air and hit them with a stick," Curtis recalled. "He'd do this for hours, playing all by himself. He had his own rules. Outs and hits were determined by where the rocks landed."

Andre always played stickball using a broomstick and a tennis ball with his uncles Curtis and John Taylor and the kids in his neighborhood. Sometimes, Andre and his uncles played a variation of the game called "Strikeout." The object was to strike out the batter. There were no called strikes, only a swing and a miss counted as a strike. "It helped me learn to make contact," Andre said. "You didn't swing wildly or you'd be out."

By the time Andre turned 10, Curtis's league had expanded into a real Little League, and Andre started traveling around Miami to play other teams. He became a powerful long ball hitter. "Andre hit some monster home runs," said Curtis. "He hit one when he was 12 that was unbelievable. It must have traveled 350 feet."

And while Andre matured as a player, he matured as a person as well. "He never had to be suspended again," said Curtis. "From that day on, he always did what he was told to do."

KIRBY PUCKETT

Outfielder

Minnesota Twins

★ ★ ★

Kirby Puckett learned to play baseball in a concrete canyon. He never played Little League ball, and didn't even play on an organized team or have a coach to teach him the fundamentals until he entered high school.

Kirby grew up in the Robert Taylor housing projects in Chicago's South Side, a neighborhood of high-rises for low-income families. From the window of his fourteenth-floor apartment, Kirby could see Comiskey Park, home of the White Sox. That was as close as he ever expected to get to the major leagues.

"There weren't any ball fields in my neighborhood—just courtyards with nothing but cement and wall-to-wall, sixteen-story buildings," recalled the Minnesota Twins' All-Star outfielder. "We didn't have any organized baseball. It was just kids against kids."

Without fields of grass or sand, Kirby and his friends had to play ball in the small cement courtyards that were bordered by the tall buildings. So the kids had to make up their own special rules.

For example, they painted squares on the walls of the buildings to mark the bases that they had to tag with their hands. Home plate was a rectangle drawn on a wall. The batter stood in front of the rectangle, and the pitcher threw a hard rubber ball. If the ball landed inside the rectangle, it was a strike. The ball bounced right back to the pitcher, so there was no need for a catcher.

Most of the time, there was room for only four players on a team. All the runs had to be scored with hits. "The buildings were far enough apart so that if you hit the other building on the fly, it was a home run," recalled Kirby. "If the ball bounced twice before it hit the wall, it was a double. If it bounced once, it was a triple."

Sometimes a well-hit ball crashed through a window. When that happened, the first thing the players did was to scatter. No one had the money to pay for a broken window.

Kirby showed signs of his incredible power at the plate when he was 11 years old and hit a home run ball that broke a third-floor window. Everybody ran, and Kirby scooted up the stairs to his apartment to hide. "The only problem was that everybody who lived in the projects knew I was the only kid strong enough to have hit the ball that far," Kirby said. "Five minutes later, there was a knock on the door and I knew I was caught. My mother made me do little jobs to earn the money to pay for that window."

But that didn't stop Kirby from playing baseball in the projects. Other than breaking that window, Kirby stayed out of trouble because he did play baseball. "During the summer, we played ball in the courtyard from the time we got up in the morning until it was dark," said Kirby.

"I didn't miss anything by not having nice fields to play on like the other kids. If I had to go back to being a kid, I'd do the same thing all over again."

Shortstop

Cincinnati Reds

★ ★ ★

Thirteen-year-old Barry Larkin deliberately got thrown out of a game because he hated to pitch.

The future Cincinnati Reds' All-Star shortstop was playing for the St. John's Eagles in a CYO league in Silverton, a suburb of Cincinnati. Barry was an all-star infielder and pitcher who had the strongest arm on the team. Although he was willing to play almost any position, he simply did not want to pitch.

"Barry was happy to get thrown out of that game," his mother, Shirley, said. "He hated pitching and didn't want to do it. He had a great arm, but his coaches had to force him to pitch. He hit several batters in his early years in Little League, and he never wanted to pitch after that.

"If Barry was forced to pitch, he pur-posely acted up, hoping to get thrown out of the game," his mother recalled. "And one time, he did get ejected because he didn't get his way."

It happened during an important game. The Eagles needed their best arm on the mound, so the coaches penciled Barry into the lineup as their starting pitcher. But Barry made it clear from the first inning that he didn't want to pitch.

After every pitch, he'd slowly walk around the mound while shuffling his feet. He'd stop and kick at the dirt for a few seconds, then move on before stopping again to do the same thing. "It was taking Barry several minutes between each pitch," his mother recalled. "The umpire walked out to the mound and asked him to stop. The umpire wanted the game to move along more quickly. Barry was slowing it down."

But Barry refused to pay any attention to the umpire. Several more times, the ump was forced to ask Barry to speed it up, but Barry simply ignored him.

In the third inning, after his team had batted and was running back on the field, Barry stalled by slowly tying his shoes while sitting on the bench. The umpire walked over and asked him to take the mound. For a minute or two, Barry ignored him before he trudged back on the field.

When Barry reached the mound, he started walking around it. After the umpire made two trips to the mound to order Barry to pitch, the fed-up ump tossed Barry out of the game.

"I was kind of happy about it," Barry recalled. "Then I looked up in the stands and saw my parents staring at me. I didn't know they were there."

Shirley and her husband, Robert, didn't say a word to Barry during the game. They didn't have to. Their frowns of disappoint-ment sent a quick message that wiped the smug smile off his face. "When Barry saw us sitting there, his face fell," his mother said. "He was happy about leaving the game until then. Our looks told him that we were very unhappy about him getting thrown out of the game."

His parents glumly watched from the bleachers as the Eagles' new pitcher was tagged with several runs and the team lost the crucial game. Afterward, nothing was said until Barry got into the family car. "I read him the riot act," his mother recalled. "I wanted to know why he had embar-rassed us and why he had quit on his team. His father and I were very angry. We gave it to Barry for a solid two weeks."

It was a lecture Barry never forgot. "My mom told me I had a responsibility to act a certain way when I was in public," Barry recalled. "I had to act properly and never get thrown out of a game. If I did, I was let-ting myself and my team down. I remem-ber my mom's words to this day, and I try to live by them."

NICK ESASKY

First
Baseman
————
Atlanta
Braves

★ ★ ★

Teaching Nick Esasky to hit and field turned into a family affair.

Almost every night, Nick, his parents, his four sisters, and his little brother went to a nearby park, where Nick spent hours hitting pitches thrown by his dad, while the rest of the family retrieved the balls.

When the future Atlanta Braves' first baseman began playing organized baseball at the age of 6 in his hometown of Carol City, Florida, he wasn't a very good player. In fact, Nick was stuck in right field because he couldn't catch pop-ups or grounders and the coach wanted him in the least important position. Fielding wasn't Nick's only problem. He couldn't hit, either.

But then his whole family pitched in to help him become a better player. "Every night after my dad came home from work, he'd grab the whole family, and we would go to the park," Nick recalled. "I would hit, my dad would pitch, and the rest of my family would field. I'd hit for an hour or two with my dad, four sisters, brother, and even my mother."

Neighbors watched the entire Esasky clan at the park: his dad, Nick Sr., a mechanic for Eastern Airlines; his mom, Flo; three older sisters, Cindy, Donna, and Kathy; his younger sister, Sonya, and his younger brother, John. "I'd have to put the younger kids far out in the field so they wouldn't get hurt," said Nick Sr. "But they didn't mind. The girls really enjoyed our nightly outings of batting practice with Nick. They didn't mind chasing the ball."

No one in the Esasky family complained about having to field for Nick. The whole family loved baseball and loved spending time together at the park. When Nick's father had to work, his mother would take the family to the park, where she would pitch to Nick.

Nick's mom also helped him with his fielding. She would play catch with him in their backyard. When no one was available, Nick would throw a tennis ball against the house and field it, or he would lie on his back and throw the ball up in the air and catch it. His fielding improved so much that by the time he was 7 years old and in his second year of little league, he was playing shortstop.

"I worked hard in my backyard to learn to field," Nick recalled. "I'd throw the ball hard against the wall and make it bounce several times on the way back to me. I made the ball go to my left and to my right. I worked on my fielding constantly."

Still, Nick's real love remained hitting, and his father continued to work on it every night with him. "All I really wanted to do was hit," Nick said. "I just got better and better at it thanks to my family. My dad wanted me to swing the bat every day, so we always went to the park."

Sometimes, Nick Sr. worked on his son's hitting immediately before Nick played in games. Other times, the whole family would be involved in Nick's batting practice before he went to his team's regular practices.

"I actually worked harder before practice than I did at practice," Nick said. "In little league, there are just too many players for any one player to get enough atten-tion. My family gave me the opportunity to learn to hit. My dad would throw the ball fairly hard to me." Although Nick seldom hit any homers, he became a contact line drive hitter.

"My dad made me the hitter I am today," Nick said. "He taught me everything I know about hitting. The rest of my family deserves a lot of the credit as well. Without them, I might still not be able to hit."

JIM ABBOTT

★ ★ ★

Nothing was going to stop Jim Abbott from playing baseball—not even the fact that he was born with a deformed right hand. Although people doubted him, Jim was determined to bat, field, and even pitch just like his buddies despite his birth defect.

"I always pictured myself as a baseball player when I was growing up," said the California Angels' inspiring pitcher. "I always told myself that I wanted to be the next Nolan Ryan. I never thought that I couldn't do it just because I had one hand."

Jim was born with only a small finger on a deformed right hand. It seemed that there was no way he could use the hand to play baseball. But his parents, Mike and Kathy, encouraged Jim to try everything that his buddies did. "Jim had tremendous courage and heart," his mother said. "We could see very early that he was determined to make it in baseball. He didn't want to be treated as if he was handicapped in any way."

Jim was lucky to start his baseball days in the Greater Flint (Michigan) Youth Baseball Program. His handicap would have prevented him from playing in many parts of the country, but Flint's policy was that anyone could join a team and that all players had to get in the game. "I always wanted to compete," Jim said. "The baseball program in Flint gave me the opportunity."

Still, there were many doubters when Jim first started playing organized baseball at the age of 9. How could a boy with only one hand hit? How could he field and throw the ball? Jim showed everyone he could do it very well. "I worked very hard,"

Jim recalled. "I felt I could play the game. The only thing that could stop me was myself."

Jim started to perfect his pitching technique. He would throw the ball left-handed with his glove resting on his deformed right hand. Once he released the pitch, he quickly would slip his left hand into the glove and be ready to field.

"I had to be able to deliver the pitch smoothly and without any interruption, then shift quickly to be ready to field," said Jim. "If I caught the ball, then I would shift the glove back under my right arm so I could get the ball out with my left hand and throw out the runner. I spent thousands of hours perfecting this." Today, Jim does it so smoothly that it looks natural.

"Believe me, there were plenty of problems doing the glove-shift at first," Jim recalled, "but I kept at it. I wanted to play baseball, so I had to perfect that technique."

He also learned how to hit with one hand and developed a strong wrist and forearm by lifting weights. By the time Jim was 11 years old, he was so skillful that he led his Little League team in hitting and was unbeaten that year as a pitcher. "Everyone sat up and took notice," Jim recalled. "I was no longer a freak. I was a player just like everyone else."

Jim kept getting better and better. Despite the fact that he hit with only one hand, he batted .427, blasted seven home runs during his senior year in high school, and was nearly untouchable as a pitcher.

"When Jim was a boy, there would be things said to him by other kids about his hand," Jim's dad said. "The kids were pretty rough on him, but we just told him to get back out there and show them he was as good as they were. None of us ever told Jim he couldn't do something. We encouraged him to try everything. Now here he is in the major leagues. It just goes to show what you can accomplish when you put your mind to it."

JESSE BARFIELD

As a little league pitcher, Jesse Barfield would get so upset when he lost that he wouldn't eat for the next two or three days!

"Finally, I had to tell him he'd have to stop pitching if he continued to take losses so hard," his mother, Annie, said. "He had to learn that baseball was a game where you couldn't always win."

The future New York Yankees' slugger grew up in Joliet, Illinois, and didn't play organized baseball until he was 12 years old. During his first year of playing for the Eastside Athletic Club, Jesse—whom his friends and relatives called "June," which was short for Junior—lost his share of games as a pitcher. With every setback, he lost his appetite.

No defeat was harder for Jesse to take than his first championship game. He was pitching in the last inning with a three-run lead against his team's biggest rival. Jesse needed only one more out to win the game. But the bases were loaded for batter Rodney Horn. There was no opponent whom Jesse wanted to beat more than Rodney. They had competed against each other in different sports for years.

"I blew the first two pitches by him for strikes," Jesse recalled. "I decided I'd throw a curve to strike him out. But Rodney had a big upper-cut swing, and he connected solidly with my curve ball." The ball sailed up, up, and away, over the left field fence. Rodney stood at the plate and admired his grand slam before trotting around the bases with the dramatic winning run.

"While he stood and watched it go, I just broke down and cried," Jesse recalled. "I cried like a baby. I never wanted to pitch again."

And for a couple of days, it looked as if he never wanted to eat again, either. Jesse went into such a deep depression that he lost his appetite. "If you can't learn to accept defeat, then you can't pitch anymore," his mom told Jesse. "You have to learn that when you go out on a baseball field and do your best, that's all you can do. If you lose, then you lose; and you go back to play another day." His mom's words finally sank in, and Jesse started eating again.

His first year in little league proved painful for another reason. In one game, Jesse batted against a particularly wild pitcher who threw very hard. "The boy couldn't find the plate," Jesse's mother recalled. "He either kept hitting everyone or walking them, but his coach wouldn't take him out of the game." That turned out to be a real sore point for Jesse—literally. The first time Jesse batted, the pitcher plunked him in the side. The next time at bat, he was hit in the upper back. Both times, Jesse was hurt, but he refused to come out of the game. The third time at bat, he was hit again in the lower back. He was in severe pain, but again he refused to leave the game.

But his mother had seen enough. "If you hit my son again," she yelled at the wild pitcher from the stands, "I'm going to come out and hit you!" The pitcher was upset at Mrs. Barfield because he wasn't trying to hit Jesse on purpose. "I scared him, and I shouldn't have done that," admitted Mrs. Barfield. "After the game, I went up to him and his parents and apologized. I ended up hugging the boy."

Then she turned her attention to her own son. She took Jesse to the emergency room for X rays because he was in so much pain. Fortunately, the X rays showed nothing was wrong; but Jesse's back was a mass of bruises, and he could hardly move for days.

Despite the heartaches and backaches, Jesse was hooked on baseball. "Ever since I was a kid, I've tried to do my best on the ball field," he said. "I can't do any more than that. I always give 100 percent; and if my team loses, I come back and give 100 percent the next day."

JEFF BRANTLEY

Pitcher
___
San
Francisco
Giants

★ ★ ★

When Jeff Brantley first started playing third base for his Little League team, he couldn't throw the ball across the infield on the fly because his arm wasn't strong enough.

"As a third baseman, Jeff was a very good fielder," said his dad, Hoke. "But his arm wasn't very strong. He couldn't make the throw to first in the air. He always bounced the ball when he threw it across the diamond."

Jeff started playing baseball at the age of 8 in Memphis, Tennessee. The future San Francisco Giants' relief pitcher was the smallest player on the team and that bothered him. "Jeff was always a small kid," his father said. "He refused even to take off his shirt because he was so small and skinny. He was afraid of the other kids laughing at him. But he had guts, and he would play with the bigger and older kids stride for stride. He didn't back down."

Jeff was determined to improve his arm strength. "How am I going to make my arm stronger?" he asked his father. "I want to play shortstop, and unless I can make the throw from the hole, I'll never get to play short."

"Your arm will get stronger as you get older," his dad replied.

But Jeff left nothing to chance. He began his own strength-improvement program. For hours at a time, he threw a rubber ball against the side of his house and caught it. This helped strengthen his arm and improve his fielding.

"Jeff would throw that ball day and night," his father said. "All you could hear in the house was the constant thump of the ball. He even chipped away the mortar between the bricks because he threw the ball against it so much."

It drove his mother, Patsy, crazy. She was always yelling at him to stop throwing the ball against the house. Jeff would stop for 10 minutes or so. Then the thump of the ball against the wall would resume. "You couldn't threaten Jeff," his father said. "Nothing would make him stop throwing the ball against the house unless he had someone else to play catch with."

By the time he was 10, Jeff's arm had become strong enough for him to play short. He could make the difficult throw from the hole and nail the runner. He was a slick-fielding shortstop who gobbled up everything that was hit near him. "Jeff was very fluid in the field," his father said. "He was a great fielder."

When Jeff was 13, he was able to work out with weights in a gym that his father had built in the family garage. "Jeff started working out diligently," his father said. "He wasn't allowed to work out with weights until he was in his teens because I didn't want him to destroy his body working out at too young an age."

When Jeff's family moved to Birmingham, Alabama, his arm had become so strong that his coaches used him as a pitcher. But Jeff really didn't like to pitch because he would get nervous on the mound. In fact, he would suffer from such a bad case of butterflies that he could never start a game. "Jeff would always be brought to the mound in the second inning," his dad recalled. "If he started, he was very nervous and would walk three or four batters. He was never nervous when he was brought into the game in the second inning. He always had good control then. It was like he was born to be a relief pitcher."

FRANK WHITE

Second Baseman

Kansas City Royals

★ ★ ★

Frank White thought that catcher was the easiest position to play—until he tried it. He quit after only three pitches!

The Kansas City Royals' All-Star infielder was a well-known little leaguer in his hometown of Kansas City. "I was a fan favorite," Frank recalled. "People liked to watch me play because I was very good. But I wasn't quite as good as I thought I was when I tried to catch."

Frank had played every position but catcher for his Hallmark Cards team in the T.B. Watkins 14-and-Under League. By the time he was 12, he was the team's slickest-fielding player. And he was cocky enough to believe that he could do anything he wanted to do on the baseball diamond.

"We didn't have very many players on our team," Frank said. "One game our regular catcher was sick, so I said I would play the position. I thought it looked easy. I figured the catcher didn't have to run around all over the field. All he had to do

was stay in one place, catch the ball, and throw it back to the pitcher."

So Frank confidently donned the catcher's gear. His batterymate didn't have any fancy pitches; the hurler just threw fast balls. Frank called for the first pitch and set up to receive it. The pitcher wheeled and threw a hard fast ball. Frank suddenly felt a twinge of fear and closed his eyes. The ball hit him smack in the head over the mask but, fortunately, right on the helmet he was wearing. There was a loud *thunk*, and the ball went bouncing all the way to the backstop. With a slight stagger, Frank retrieved the ball and threw it back to the pitcher. "I was a little woozy," Frank recalled. "The pitch hit me square in the head. My helmet saved me."

After clearing his head, Frank called for the next pitch. It came roaring in, and Frank closed his eyes again. *Thunk!* This time, the ball hit him on the left shin guard. "That hurt my knee," Frank recalled. "I limped out from behind the plate and threw the ball back to the pitcher. Now I was sore in two places."

Frank told himself that if he'd just keep his eyes open, he'd be able to catch the ball and wouldn't get hurt. But those first two pitches had made him gun-shy. His confidence was shot.

The third pitch came zooming in, and the batter swung and missed. Once again, Frank had closed his eyes. *Thunk!* "The third pitch hit the shin guard covering my right knee," Frank recalled. "Now, both knees and my head hurt. I'd had enough."

Frank called time and limped back to the bench. Then, to everyone's surprise, he took off his catching gear and told the coach, "Catching is not for me." Three pitches and Frank's catching career was over.

Frank had never quit on a baseball field. "For a while, Frank was torn up over that game," recalled his father, Frank Sr. "He thought he could do anything, but he found out he couldn't catch. It was the first time Frank couldn't do something in baseball."

After that game, Frank was still willing to play any position on the field—except catcher. "I didn't like catching at all," Frank said. "I thought it was the easiest job in baseball, but I found out it was the worst. Those three pitches beat me up. I couldn't have taken any more. My body was too hurt to go on. I've never tried catching again."

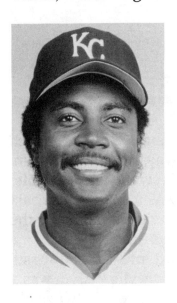

ALVIN DAVIS

First
Baseman
—
Seattle
Mariners

★ ★ ★

Alvin Davis learned how to hit by playing whiffle ball with his two older brothers—and by using an old real estate sign to determine the strike zone.

"If the whiffle ball hit the sign, it was a strike," Alvin recalled. "There were never any arguments in our games. The sign determined strikes and balls; and certain areas of the field determined whether or not a hit was a single, double, triple, or home run."

The Seattle Mariners' first baseman credits his phenomenal batting eye to the games he played in his yard with his brothers, Mike and Mel, in Lakeview Terrace, California. "We played three-man games," said Alvin, who began playing when he was 6 years old. "The games taught me to be a good, disciplined hitter."

If the ball was hit into the street, which was about 90 feet away, it was a home run. Hitting over the sidewalk was a triple; onto the driveway was a double; and past the pitcher was a single. Of course, if the ball was caught, it was an out.

"The boys would play for hours," recalled Alvin's mom, Mylie. "Alvin was a chubby little kid, but he could always hit. His brothers made an athlete out of him." Mike was 5 years older than Alvin, and Mel was 7 years older. They didn't care that Alvin was only 6; they included him in all their games. "They didn't throw as hard to me as they threw to each other," Alvin said. "But they still made the whiffle ball curve, knuckle, and do other things. It helped me learn to hit different pitches. It's hard enough to hit a whiffle ball, anyway.

But we'd make it even harder. We'd put rocks in the ball, dent it on one side, and do other things to it to make it dip and dive."

Above all, Alvin learned the strike zone in those games with the help of a real estate sign. When the Davis family moved to Lakeview Terrace, the real estate agent had failed to remove the "For Sale" sign that hung in the front yard. When the house was bought, the sign was taken out of the ground and placed against the front wall of the house.

"We were going to throw the sign away," Alvin's mom said, "but the boys had other ideas. They figured it was perfect for baseball."

The sign hung on two posts and was about 2 feet by 2 feet. The batter would stand in front of it. If the pitch hit the sign, it was a called strike. One brother would pitch while the other played the field. When the batter made three outs, he would go out into the field. The fielder would become the pitcher, and the pitcher would become the batter. "We didn't need an umpire," said Alvin. "The pinging sound of the ball hitting the sign let you know it was a strike."

The whiffle ball game was the idea of Alvin's dad, Bill, who was afraid the boys would break windows if they used a regular ball.

Alvin fondly remembers his years of playing whiffle ball in the backyard with his brothers, and he credits his success today to the games he played in Lakeview Terrace.

"Those games gave me the discipline I have at the plate today," Alvin says. "In the major leagues, I'm known for not chasing bad pitches. But it all goes back to the days when I played whiffle ball with a real estate sign for a strike zone."

BILL LANDRUM

Pitcher

Pittsburgh Pirates

★ ★ ★

When Bill Landrum was a Little League pitcher in Columbia, South Carolina, he threw fast balls—and temper tantrums.

Whenever an umpire made a call that Bill didn't like, the future Pittsburgh Pirates' hurler would rant and rave. Then he would storm off the mound and refuse to pitch. "If the umpire called a ball that Bill thought was a strike, he'd go berserk," Bill's mom, Rose Marie, recalled. "Bill would throw down his glove, stomp off the mound, and scream."

Bill was 9 years old and playing for the Eau Claire Lions when he first displayed his terrible temper. "I'm not pitching anymore!" Bill shouted after disputing an umpire's call. Bill slammed his glove to the ground and yelled, "The umpire is no good, and I won't pitch!" After several minutes of screaming and hollering, Bill picked up his glove and moved to shortstop. He simply refused to pitch to another batter in the game. He pulled the same childish stunt several times. Surprisingly, Bill's coach always let him get away with it.

After watching several exhibitions of Bill's temper, his mother finally laid down the law. She collared Bill and his coach and said sternly, "Bill, you're out there to play ball and not to make a fool of yourself. Coach, if Bill walks off the mound and refuses to pitch again, he's through with baseball. I won't allow him to play anymore."

Rose Marie's strong words got the immediate attention of Bill's coach. But for Bill, it took a little bit longer before his mom's words sunk in. He threw a few more temper tantrums on the mound, but each time his coach refused to let him move to shortstop. Either Bill had to calm down and pitch or else leave the game. Bill soon realized that he had to put a lid on his temper if he ever hoped to play a full game. Besides, he had to face his mother, who was watching him from the stands.

"Bill knew I meant business," his mother said. "If he didn't control his temper, he was through with baseball. Thankfully, he learned to overcome this bad habit."

For the next four years, Bill never lost his cool on the mound—not until that fateful game for the Pony League state championship when he was 13 years old. Pitching for the Eau Claire Exchange, Bill wanted desperately to beat the other team because many of its players were on the club that had whipped his Little League team in the state finals the year before.

"I wanted to beat these guys badly," Bill recalled. "We felt we had been cheated out of a victory by a bad call the year before when an umpire called a hit that had bounced through a hole in the fence a home run. It cost us the game."

On the morning of the big game, Bill's dad took him in the backyard and taught him how to throw a quick pitch from the stretch position. "We worked on it for hours," Bill said. "He wanted me to have something to use in case I needed one quick strike in a jam."

Bill got into a jam in the bottom of the last inning with the game tied 1-1. Fielding lapses by his teammates had allowed a runner to get to third. Bill needed a strikeout to end the threat and send the game into extra innings. So Bill tried the quick pitch. It worked. Or so he thought. The umpire immediately called a balk and waved in the winning run.

"It's a good pitch! It's not a balk!" Bill yelled at the umpire. "Everyone knows it was legit." He flailed his arms and shouted until he was hoarse, but it did no good. The umpire refused to change his mind, and Bill's team lost the state championship over a questionable balk call.

Although Bill lost his temper, this time his mother had reason to forgive him.

MICKEY TETTLETON

Mickey Tettleton sharpened his batting stroke as a kid by hitting baseballs that he made out of newspapers and electrical tape.

The future Baltimore Orioles' All-Star catcher had to make his own baseballs after his parents warned him about breaking windows in his neighborhood in Oklahoma City, Oklahoma.

"I didn't start playing with a real baseball for years," Mickey said. "I was raised in the middle of the city, and there were a lot of windows around. My mom and dad wanted to keep the neighbors as friends, so they told me I couldn't use a real baseball around the house."

From the time Mickey was 5 years old, he began making his own balls by crumpling up newspaper and wrapping it in tape until it was about 3 inches in diameter. He'd use any kind of tape, but he preferred black electrical tape. "We never had any tape in the house," his mother, Virginia, complained. "Mickey would use every roll of it."

For about ten years, Mickey made his own baseballs and had a unique way of playing with them out in the yard. "Mickey had a favorite beige plastic bat that he would use to hit," his mother said. He even had the handle of the bat taped. Mickey would throw the taped newspaper ball up on the roof, then quickly take a right-handed batting stance under the eaves. He couldn't see the ball until it came off the roof. When it fell, he would hit it.

Because the ball was only newspaper, it couldn't go very far, and there was no danger of it breaking anything. However, Mickey could hit it over 100 feet. "As Mickey got older, he hit the ball farther," his mother recalled. "He used to hit it over the neighbors' fence and up against their house. They didn't mind, because the taped ball couldn't hurt anything."

Mickey used to make dozens of these taped balls in a week. "No matter where you went in our house," his mother said, "you would find one of Mickey's taped balls. They were everywhere."

Mickey had developed such a good stroke from hitting his homemade baseballs that he became one of the best hitters in his local Little League. When he was 12 years old, Mickey was picked to pitch and play third base on an all-star team, the Rufnex, from Oklahoma City. They went on to win the United States championship of Boy's Baseball, which played by major league baseball rules. Mickey's team then won the right to compete in Mexico City against seven other teams for the international championship.

The Rufnex won the international championship of Boy's Baseball, although Mickey didn't get to play as much as he hoped. He had come down with Montezuma's Revenge, a stomach virus that Americans frequently suffer from after drinking the water in Mexico.

"Even though I was sick, it was a great experience for me," said Mickey. "I got to meet and play against boys from all over the world. We played in Mexico's Olympic Stadium and lived in the Olympic Village. It was an awesome experience. I'll never forget it."

CRAIG BIGGIO

Catcher
—
Houston Astros

★ ★ ★

For years, the sound of thunder and the flash of lightning has triggered haunting memories for Craig Biggio.

When the Houston Astros' catcher was a teenager, he witnessed a heart-wrenching tragedy on the baseball field: One of his teammates was struck and killed by lightning.

"It took me five years to get over my total fear of lightning," Craig recalled. "If I saw lightning in the distance, I wanted to get off the ball field immediately."

Craig was 16 years old and playing in the Connie Mack League in Kings Park, Long Island, when the tragic incident occurred. His team had won all twenty of its games, but it was losing on this particular day by four runs in the fifth inning when a light sprinkle began to fall. "The rain was just a drizzle," Craig said. "It wasn't enough to stop the game. It wasn't accompanied by any lightning, although way off in the distance we could see lightning and hear thunder."

Craig was normally a shortstop for his team. But on this day, Adriano Martinez was playing short, and Craig was at second base. Adriano was the nephew of former major leaguer Manny Mota.

"We were actually admiring the lightning display in the distance," Craig recalled. "It was so far away that we didn't think anything of it." Although the drizzle had stopped, a big black cloud hung over the field. But neither the umpires nor the coaches thought the game should be interrupted just because of a storm cloud.

But then, with startling suddenness, a thunderous bolt of lightning slammed into the infield. Craig was knocked a foot off the ground and then lost consciousness for a few seconds. "I remember hearing the loud thunderbolt and being knocked off my feet," Craig recalled. "But what I'll never forget is the feeling of a warm sensation running up the back of my legs and my spine." He was feeling the high voltage of the nearby deadly lightning bolt.

When Craig regained consciousness, he found himself curled up like a baby on the ground. He knew immediately that lightning had struck near him. "When I awoke and started to look around, the first thing I saw was Adriano lying on the ground," Craig said. "His left sock was on fire."

Craig yelled, "Adriano's leg is burning!" And then he joined the rush to his fallen teammate. It was obvious that Adriano had been hit by lightning, and a quick check of his pulse showed that his heart had stopped. Immediately, the emergency squad was called, and a coach administered CPR. They worked on Adriano for nearly an hour, but tragically they couldn't revive him. Adriano was pronounced dead.

"We were all shocked," Craig recalled. "All I could think of was that I could've been killed since I normally played short-stop."

The team voted to cancel the rest of the season. "No one felt like playing anymore," said Craig. "We probably would have been champions, but who cared? It was a small thing compared to Adriano's death."

Over the next few years, Craig became extremely fearful of lightning. "It's not hard to develop a fear of lightning when a friend is killed 10 feet away from you by it," he said. "For five years, I would seek shelter the moment I saw lightning in the distance. I couldn't sleep during a stormy night."

The sight of Adriano lying there with his sock burning still haunts Craig today, although he has overcome his fear of lightning. Now Craig has a warning to all young baseball players: "When there's a storm around, get off the field. Lightning is dangerous and can kill you. Don't think you are safe just because it isn't hitting where you are at that moment."

DWIGHT GOODEN

Pitcher
___
New
York
Mets

★ ★ ★

Dwight Gooden felt so uncomfortable playing in front of his parents that once when he was 8 years old, he walked off the diamond in the middle of a game after he spotted them in the stands.

The future strikeout king of the New York Mets was playing shortstop for Belmont Heights in his hometown of Tampa, Florida, when shyness and nervousness dampened his desire to play.

"I saw my parents sitting up in the stands, and I didn't want to play anymore," Dwight recalled. "I was scared to play in front of them. I was afraid I'd do something wrong on the field, and I didn't want to be embarrassed in front of them."

The game had gone into the third inning before Dwight first noticed his mother, Ella Mae, and his father, Dan, sitting in the bleachers cheering him on. There was one out, and a batter was at the plate.

"Suddenly, Dwight looked into the stands and saw us sitting there," his father recalled. "He stared straight at us for a sec-

ond or two, then walked right off the field. Everyone was shocked."

The umpire called time out and walked over to the bench where Dwight was talking with his bewildered coach. "Dwight told his coach that he didn't want to play anymore," recalled his dad. "He refused to go back on the field, and the coach had to put in another shortstop. Dwight wouldn't tell the coach why he didn't want to play anymore."

Concerned that something had happened to their son, Dwight's parents came down to talk with him. He told them that he was all right, but he wouldn't tell them why he refused to play.

"Later we discovered the reason," Dwight's dad said. "Dwight didn't want to play in front of his mother or me because he was nervous and embarrassed. He didn't want us to watch him play."

The coach understood, even though Dwight's parents were hurt. They wanted to watch their son play. "We sort of came to a compromise," his dad said. "We would go to the games but sit where Dwight couldn't easily spot us."

Dwight agreed to the plan and began playing again. But it was difficult because he sometimes saw his parents in the stands. "He hated to make eye contact with me or his dad," Dwight's mom said. "He'd get a real scared look on his face when he saw us, and I could see him get nervous."

It took Dwight a few years before he could play in front of his parents without feeling awkward. "I had to keep telling Dwight there was nothing to be nervous about," his dad said. "We just wanted him to have a good time and to do his best. We didn't care if he made some mistakes."

By the time Dwight was 12 years old, he had become a tremendous ballplayer and a tough competitor. In fact, he became so intense that he would break down and cry whenever his team lost. "Dwight expected everyone to play as hard and as well as he did," his father explained. "He'd get angry at his teammates if they fell short of his expectations, but he didn't say anything to them. He would just cry if they lost the game."

Dwight reached his lowest point in little league when he was 12 and playing third base in a championship game. With two out and the winning run on third in the last inning, the batter hit a ground ball to Dwight. But Dwight mishandled the ball and allowed the winning run to score. "Dwight broke down and cried," his father recalled. "He kept repeating, 'I lost the game.' I told him it wasn't true, that in baseball you win as a team, and you lose as a team. He just kept crying."

Dwight still possesses that kind of intensity in the major leagues. He hates to lose. And he still is uncomfortable when his parents are in the stands watching him. "Believe it or not," Dwight said, "I'm still nervous about playing in front of my parents. It doesn't paralyze me anymore, but I still try to do more than I should just because they are watching."

MARK McGWIRE

<table>
<tr><td>
**First
Baseman**

**Oakland
Athletics**

★ ★ ★
</td><td></td></tr>
</table>

Oakland Athletics power-hitting All-Star Mark McGwire was destined to play for the A's. After all, he started playing for the Athletics when he was 10 years old.

Actually, Mark played for a Little League team called the Athletics for three years. He was a slugger and a leader on the A's, just like he is now. Even the uniforms were the same as he wears now—gold, green, and white.

"It makes you wonder," said his dad, John. "Here he was playing on a team with the same name and colors as the one he plays for in the major leagues."

Mark almost didn't get the opportunity to play in Little League. When he was 8 years old and eligible for his first year of organized baseball in his hometown of Claremont, California, his parents wouldn't let him play. "I had heard a lot of criticism about Little League parents and how they interfere with the kids' fun," said his dad. "I thought Mark was too young to handle the pressure. So I told Mark, 'Let's cool it as far as baseball is concerned for this year.' Mark was pretty upset because all his buddies were joining Little League and he couldn't. He finally accepted it. I wanted the game to be fun for Mark."

After a year of looking into it, Mark's dad saw that the local Little League was well run. He was so impressed that he wound up becoming a member of the league's board of directors and eventually a coach.

When he was 9, Mark finally got to play in a league for 8- and 9-year-olds, and quickly he established himself as one of his team's best hitters.

The following year, when he played for the Athletics in "the majors" (Little League's division for boys ages 10 to 12), Mark really blossomed. For the first time, he got to wear a real uniform just like his major league counterparts, with socks and stirrups and cleats. Now he felt he belonged.

Mark was so excited that he could hardly sleep the night before his first game for the Athletics. When he arrived at the park, he took hundreds of practice swings in an effort to get rid of some of his nervous energy. Finally, it was game time. He stepped into the batter's box, dug his shoes into the dirt, and waited for the pitch. A fast ball flew over the heart of the plate, and Mark whipped his bat around. He knew by the sound of the bat hitting the ball that he had given it a ride. The ball sailed over the right fielder's head, and Mark raced around the bases for a home run!

He was so happy, he felt like shouting for joy. But he kept his cool. The only damper to his season-opening homer was that his parents weren't there to see it. Even though they had been to all his games the previous year, they missed this one because they had won a free cruise in a contest.

"I had to wait a whole week before I could break the great news to them," Mark said. "When they got back from their trip and pulled up the driveway, I ran out to the car; and without even saying hi, I told them all about that first home run."

From that game on, there was no stopping Mark. He led the league in homers that year and was undefeated as a pitcher. "In fact, in the three years he pitched in the league, he never lost a single game," said his dad.

When he wasn't pitching, Mark played shortstop. "He was a field general out on the diamond," said his dad. "Mark had a tremendous feel for the game at an early age. He read everything he could get his hands on about baseball and became a student of the game. On the field, he positioned his teammates for each particular batter."

After watching Mark play several times, a rival coach told Mark's parents, "Mark is going to put Claremont on the map someday. He's the best player ever to come out of this town."

The coach was so right.

JOHN KRUK

When John Kruk was a youngster, he had to learn how to hit to the opposite field. Otherwise, he would have almost always made an out in backyard baseball games.

Because so few kids lived in his hometown of Keyser, West Virginia, there were usually only four players on the field during pickup games. "We had a pitcher, an infielder, an outfielder, and a batter," recalled the Philadelphia Phillies' outfielder. "Everyone but me was a right-handed batter. So for all the other batters, the fielders lined up on the left side of second base. If the batter hit the ball to the right side of second base, it was an out."

John was the only left-handed hitter in town. At first, the fielders moved to the right side of second when he batted. If John hit the ball to the left side of second, he was out. "But that ended after a month or so," John recalled. "It was just too hot for the fielders to move every time I came up. The other players refused to do it." So John was forced to hit the ball to the left side and play by the same rules as all the right-handed batters.

By the age of 10, John was an expert at hitting to the opposite field. In addition to handling a bat well, John pitched, while his brother, Larry, caught on the local Little League team, the Keyser Giants. The team was coached by their father, Moe, who used their backyard as a practice field.

"The kids would come from all over town to play in our backyard," said John's dad. "Our house was sports central for Keyser." The Kruks laid out a baseball field on the acre of vacant land they owned behind their house. The diamond featured a real home plate, bases made of coffee sacks full of sand, and a pitcher's rubber. "There were no fences," John's mother, Lena, recalled. "But it was at least 200 feet to the trees. We didn't start losing baseballs in there until John reached his teens."

Usually, there were only a few kids who played at any one time; but on especially hot days, the Kruks' backyard would be filled with as many as fourteen kids—just about all the boys in Keyser. "We loved those days," said John's dad, "because there were enough kids to field two teams of seven each. On those days, John could hit the ball anywhere on the field."

There was still a problem, though. The kids showed up on the very hot days because they knew they could use the Kruks' swimming pool. "Some kids would play baseball for only a few minutes," Lena recalled. "Then they would jump in the pool and not come out. Soon, John was back to hitting the ball to the left side of the field because only a few kids were still playing baseball while the rest swam.

Despite the heat, John and his brother were always out on the field. They just loved baseball. "I couldn't even plant a tree in part of the yard," John's mother recalled. "If I did, I would have been accused of trying to prevent the boys from playing ball. The regular field was strictly off-limits for any gardening."

Today, John is thankful for being forced to hit to the opposite field. "When I was young, it eventually became natural for me to hit the ball to left since my friends in the field weren't about to move to the right side," John said. "When I got into professional baseball, I didn't have any trouble at all hitting to left. I was already used to hitting that way."

VINCE COLEMAN

Outfielder

St. Louis Cardinals

★ ★ ★

Vince Coleman hit the only grand slam of his life when he was in the tenth grade—and it beat his former teammates, who didn't think he was good enough to play with them.

The future St. Louis Cardinals' All-Star outfielder grew up in Jacksonville, Florida, in a neighborhood known for raising top athletes. Several professional football players developed their competitive spirit there, including his cousin Greg Coleman of the Minnesota Vikings, Harold Carmichael of the Philadelphia Eagles, and Booby Clark of the Cincinnati Bengals. "I wanted to be like them, only I wanted to do it in baseball," recalled Vince.

"The big thing in our neighborhood was the bragging rights. You had to outdo the other guys—strike them out, steal a base, hit a home run. That way, when you went to school the next day, you had something to talk about, and everyone knew you were the top dog in the neighborhood."

Baseball occupied Vince's free time from morning until night. In Little League,

he pitched and played every position in the infield and won the league's batting title. Every year, he led his team to victory in the all-star game.

The real test of who was best in the neighborhood came when Vince and his buddies tried out for the Paxson Junior High baseball team in the ninth grade. To his shock, Vince was cut from the squad. Although he was crushed, he continued to play hard in sandlot games. The next year, when all the players from junior high moved up to Paxson Senior High, Vince transferred to Paxson's arch rival, Raines High School. "Since all my friends went to Paxson, they used to get all over me about not making the junior high team," Vince recalled. "They said I wouldn't make the team in high school, either." But they were wrong. Vince earned the job as Raines' starting shortstop.

Vince was considered a traitor by his neighborhood friends for going to school at Raines. They constantly kidded him about his choice of schools and when

Vince made the Raines baseball team, the kidding got worse. "Everyone said that the Raines team must be lousy if I could make it," Vince recalled. "They constantly reminded me that I hadn't been good enough to make the junior high team the year before, and that the same players had moved up to Paxson's high school team. They said if I'd stayed at Paxson, I wouldn't have made the senior high team, either."

Vince had a big incentive to win when Raines played Paxson for the first time. The game was played at Paxson, where the stands were filled with his neighborhood friends and former classmates. They booed Vince when he took the field in a Raines uniform. "In the Paxson dugout, the players were laughing," Vince recalled. "They were making insulting comments about me playing for Raines."

Vince didn't do much with the bat during the game, and it seemed as though the Paxson fans had every right to think Vince wasn't good enough.

But in the final inning, Vince was given the opportunity to make them all eat their words. He came to bat with his team trailing 6-3. There were two outs, and the bases were loaded. The first two pitches to Vince were strikes, and the Paxson fans were hooting and hollering at him. But Vince didn't let them bother him. He just dug his cleats deeper into the dirt of the batter's box.

On the next pitch, the Paxson pitcher tried to slip a fast ball by Vince on the inside corner. But Vince swung with all his might and belted the pitch over the center field wall.

It was a game-winning, in-your-face, grand-slam home run!

"What a tremendous thrill it was," Vince recalled. "I was floating on air as I ran around the bases. The whole stadium was quiet. I'd managed to shut up all my critics."

Vince was happy to win the game, but he was especially excited to have hit a grand slam to win it. He says it's the only grand slam he has ever hit. "I was well aware that I had hit it against the guys whose team I couldn't make the year before," Vince said. "I showed them that they had made a big mistake."

KEVIN MITCHELL

As a little leaguer, Kevin Mitchell loved to catch so much that he went to drastic lengths to avoid playing other positions. Once, after the coach ordered him to play left field, a pouting Kevin deliberately dropped an easy fly ball in protest that cost his team the game.

"It was the wrong thing to do," admitted the San Francisco Giants' All-Star slugger. "I was a stubborn kid back then. All I wanted to do was catch. I loved to put on the mask and shins and run the show from behind the plate. I never wanted to play anywhere else."

Kevin and his brother, Tom, who was a year younger, grew up in San Diego, where they played baseball the year round. In little league, Kevin was the catcher and hitting star on the Angels. "The thing I loved the most was the home-plate collision with the runner. I enjoyed the contact. No one—and I mean no one—ever knocked the ball from my hands."

But Kevin's burning desire to catch once clouded his judgment so much that he cost his team a crushing defeat.

During an all-star game, Kevin, for reasons which he never explained, didn't show up until after the game had started. Nevertheless, Coach Bill Wells decided to let Kevin play because the team needed Kevin's power hitting.

"You can put me in to catch now," Kevin told Wells.

But the coach shook his head and said, "No, we've got a catcher for this game. You can play left field."

"I don't want to play left field," Kevin protested.

"But you have to," the coach declared.

"Okay," Kevin snapped angrily. "You can stick me out there. But I'm gonna drop the first ball that comes my way."

The coach didn't believe him and sent him into the game. Kevin didn't immediately carry through on his threat because no balls were hit to him over the next few innings. At the plate, Kevin was outstanding. He belted a triple and a home run to put his team ahead 5-3. But whenever he took his position out in left field, Kevin continued to sulk.

In the last inning, with Kevin's team still ahead by two runs, the opposing club loaded the bases with one out. Then it happened. The batter swatted a high fly to deep left field. Kevin drifted back, nestled under the ball, caught it—and then deliberately dropped it! The ball rolled all the way to the fence as the tying and winning runs crossed the plate.

"Kevin had the ball in his mitt and just turned his glove over," recalled Tom, who was playing second base. "There was nothing we could do about it. We knew he was still mad over not being allowed to catch. But no one—not even the coach—said a word to him because he would have exploded in anger."

Kevin stalked off the field and headed straight home. "He was such a stubborn boy," recalled his grandmother, Josie Whitfield. "He wouldn't talk about anything for the rest of the day. Eventually, though, he learned to change his attitude. He knew he had to play for the good of the team and that sometimes you have to do things you don't like, but you do them anyway because it will help the team."

Added Kevin, "What I did in that all-star game wasn't right. It was selfish, and I learned my lesson. You have to be a team player in baseball. On that day, I wasn't. I let my love for catching get in the way."

What's so ironic is that the position Kevin hated to play as a little leaguer—left field—is now the very same position that he plays so well in the major leagues!

LONNIE SMITH

Outfielder

Atlanta Braves

★ ★ ★

Lonnie Smith was so furious over an umpire's call during a Little League game that he stripped off his uniform in the middle of the field in protest!

The future Atlanta Braves' outfielder angrily stomped off the diamond dressed only in his underpants, socks, and baseball shoes while the crowd—which included his parents—watched in stunned silence.

What made his actions even more embarrassing was that the umpire had made the right call.

"I didn't like the umpire's decision," Lonnie recalled. "So after the inning was over, I went out to my position at shortstop and decided I didn't want to play anymore. I sat down and took my baseball uniform off."

Lonnie, then 11 years old, was an all-star shortstop for the Yankees in his hometown of Compton, California. There were always big crowds at El Segundo Park when the Yankees played because Lonnie was a favorite of the fans. But in one memorable game, Lonnie did something that shocked everyone.

"Lonnie hated to be outdone by anyone," his dad, Andrew, said. "The batter before Lonnie hit a towering home run. So Lonnie went up to bat determined to do the same. He hit the ball hard, but unfortunately it went over the fence on one bounce."

Lonnie saw the ball go over the fence, but he didn't see it bounce first. So with a beaming face, Lonnie circled the bases, thinking that he had hit a round-tripper. But when he reached home plate, the umpire ordered him back to second base because it was a ground rule double.

"Lonnie screamed at the umpire," his dad said. "He didn't want to go back to second base. Lonnie felt he should have had a home run just like the hitter before him. The coach had to come out to calm him down, and finally Lonnie returned to second. But he was very angry."

Lonnie was still steaming when the side was retired. He went to the bench and retrieved his glove before walking slowly to his position. But Lonnie didn't stop when he reached the infield. Instead, he walked onto the outfield grass behind second, sat down, and started taking off his clothes.

"The bleachers were full," Lonnie recalled. "But I didn't care. I was angry because I felt the umpire had made a bad call. I took my uniform off, and I began walking home in my underwear."

The sight of their son stripping off his pants, shirt, and baseball stirrups in the middle of the field shocked and angered Lonnie's parents. "It was terribly embarrassing," Lonnie's dad said. "All we could do was sit there and watch. Everyone was stunned by Lonnie's actions, and then they started sneaking peeks at us to see how we would react. We just sat there for a while, and then we went after Lonnie, who had started to walk home."

Before Lonnie's dad left the ball park, he marched up to the Yankees' coach and announced that Lonnie would not be allowed to play in the upcoming all-star game because of his childish behavior. When his parents found Lonnie walking home in his underpants, they ordered him into the car, where his father told Lonnie of his punishment.

Lonnie took his father's decision hard, even though he knew he was wrong. "My dad told me that I had to accept what the umpire said if I wanted to play baseball," Lonnie recalled. "I realized I shouldn't have lost my temper. But I was really hurt that my dad wasn't going to let me play in the all-star game."

Lonnie received a reprieve when his coach came over to the house and begged his father to let Lonnie play. The coach suggested that Lonnie's dad think up another punishment. "I agreed because underneath it all I wanted Lonnie to play," his dad recalled. "So I gave him the second worst punishment I could give him. I didn't allow him to watch TV for a week, and Lonnie loved TV second only to baseball."

Lonnie promised his dad he would always accept the umpire's call. "I knew I was wrong," Lonnie recalled. "I promised never to do it again. Since I've been in the major leagues, I have broken that promise at times; but whenever I do, my dad is quick to remind me of my promise."

BOBBY THIGPEN

Pitcher

Chicago
White
Sox

★ ★ ★

Bobby Thigpen wasn't going to let a little thing like a cast on his leg stop him from playing baseball. He played an entire sandlot game on crutches!

The Chicago White Sox' All-Star relief pitcher grew up in the small rural town of Aucilla, Florida, where kids played all day in their bare feet in the summer.

One day, when Bobby was 12 years old, he was running barefoot to his grandparents' house. "He was running across some railroad tracks," recalled his mother, Donna Smith. "He tripped and fell, and landed on a broken glass quart jar. The jagged glass cut a vein on top of his right foot and an artery above his right knee. He just about bled to death." Bobby was rushed to the emergency room, where they stitched him up and put on a cast from

his knee to his toes. For the next few weeks, Bobby had to hobble around on crutches.

A few days after the accident, Bobby and his family were visiting his grandparents. He was sitting on the front porch talking with the adults when he saw his cousins and their neighborhood friends grab a bat and ball, and head for the field in front of the house.

"Bobby never turned down a chance to play ball," recalled his mom. "He got up on his crutches and went out to join them because he didn't want to miss out on the fun. His grandfather hollered at him, 'Son, have you lost your mind?' Bobby just smiled. He grabbed a bat and parked himself at the plate. He leaned the crutches against himself and swung at the pitch and got a hit. Then he grabbed his crutches and hobbled down on one foot to first base. Bobby got several more hits before the day was out. He even played in the outfield on crutches."

Bobby's grandfather, J.B. Thomas, known affectionately as "Pops" by the grandchildren, couldn't help but admire Bobby's spunk. "Pops was Bobby's idol," said his mother. "They were very close." But even Pops didn't know just how much baseball meant to Bobby.

Pops, who was the local sheriff, owned a farm a few miles down the road and often halted the sandlot games whenever he needed the grandkids' help feeding the cows.

"One day," recalled Bobby's mom, "Pops stopped a game for feeding time, and called Bobby over to the porch and said, 'Son, you've got to learn to do something besides playing ball. Do you think you will ever make a living playing baseball? Now let's go down there and feed these cows. This is what puts our bread and butter on the table.' Bobby bowed his head, didn't say a word, and hopped on the truck to go help Pops feed the cows.

"Now here Bobby is making his living playing baseball. It's too bad that Pops died before Bobby made it to the big leagues. Boy, would Pops have been proud."

BILL DORAN

For two years in a row, Bill Doran was one strike away from pitching his team to the Little League championship of Cincinnati. Incredibly, both times he gave up a disastrous game-winning home run—to the same batter!

"Both years, a kid named Johnny Miller hit a three-run homer off me in the bottom of the sixth inning," recalled Bill, who was traded from the Houston Astros to the Cincinnati Reds in 1990. "We were one out away from winning the championship when Miller hit his home runs."

Bill was the top pitcher for Interchemical, a team from Seven Hills, a Cincinnati suburb where he grew up. The first year that Interchemical played Toy Center for the championship, 8-year-old Bill was breezing along with a 2-0 lead in the last inning. "Bill was really firing the ball," recalled his dad, Bill Sr., who coached the team. "He was mowing down the batters."

Bill got into a little trouble and allowed the first two men in the inning to reach base on a scratch hit and a walk. But he recovered and struck out the next two batters. With two out, the opposing first baseman, Johnny Miller, came to bat. Miller was a left-handed hitter who hadn't gotten a hit off Bill during the whole season.

Bill whipped the first two pitches by Miller for strikes. On the next pitch, Miller hit a towering drive over the center fielder's head. Since there were no fences on the field, everything had to be run out. The ball rolled almost all the way to the mound of the diamond on another field. Miller scored easily, and his three-run homer won the game—and crushed Bill's spirit. "It was the end of the world," Bill recalled. "I stood on the mound and cried. It seemed like my world had come crumbling down."

Bill's father was also disappointed, but he was determined his son would learn something from the game. Recalled his father, "I told him that was baseball. It was what made the game so great. One minute, you're winning, the next, you're losing. If he wanted to play baseball, he had to learn that there would be days he would lose. He just had to bounce back and try to win the next game."

The next year, Bill was confident when his team faced Toy Center again for the championship. "Once more it came down to the bottom of the sixth," Bill recalled. "There were two outs and two on, and we were leading 5-3."

Bill's nemesis from the year before, Johnny Miller, stepped up to the plate. Bill had silenced Miller's bat throughout the game, and he felt sure he could do it again.

On the first pitch, Miller swung and missed badly. The second pitch was a called strike. Miller stepped out of the batter's box and composed himself. Then, he stepped back in, ready to face Bill.

"I was totally confident," Bill recalled. "I knew I had his number." Once again, Bill was just one pitch away from winning the city championship. All he had to do was get this next pitch by Miller, and Bill would finally get his revenge for the devastating homer he had served up the previous year.

But like a horrifying instant replay, Miller swung on Bill's next pitch—and blasted it even farther than he had the year before. Bill just turned and watched the ball sail over the center fielder's head and roll near the spot where last year's gopher ball had ended up. "I turned around and looked at my dad in the dugout," Bill recalled. "Then, I threw my arms up in the air and shrugged. My only thought was that Johnny had got me again."

On the bench, his dad was heartbroken, but he realized Bill had learned a valuable lesson from the year before. "Bill gave me a little smile," his dad recalled. "It was like he thought he had done his best and Johnny Miller had beaten him again.

There wasn't anything else he could do about it."

Bill had indeed learned his lesson. "Those games taught me that even though you lose, you still must go on and play again," said Bill.

Trying hard to forget those two crushing, dream-dashing homers, Bill pitched his team to its third straight appearance in the city championship the following year. This time, Interchemical won. But Bill didn't pitch against Toy Center in the championship game. Another pitcher on Interchemical had beaten Johnny Miller's team earlier in the playoffs.

"There was no chance Miller was going to beat me three times in a row," Bill said. "But if he had, I would have just gone on and played. In baseball, there's always another game."

DAVID CONE

David Cone once knocked out an umpire with a wild throw during a Little League game. The future New York Mets' pitcher was so scared that he dashed off the field and had to be coaxed into coming back to play.

"I ran into the dugout," David recalled. "I thought the umpire was going to beat me up."

David was 9 years old and playing third base for the Armco Steelers in Kansas City when he experienced his most embarrassing moment. At the start of the third inning, David's team took the field. While the pitcher was warming up, the first baseman was tossing ground balls to the infielders.

"I fielded a grounder from the first base-man and threw hard across to first base," David recalled. "It was a wild throw, and it hit the umpire squarely in the forehead." The ump, a middle-aged man, wasn't looking at the time because he was partially turned away, talking to someone in the opposing team's dugout.

"The sound of the ball hitting the umpire's head was very loud," David said. "It made a booming sound. The umpire immediately fell down and was momentarily knocked out. When I saw the umpire fall, I ran straight for my dugout. I thought he was going to beat me up when he revived."

Fearfully, David watched from the dugout as fans, players, and coaches ran to help the umpire. When the ump was revived, he sat on the ground, holding his head. Finally, he managed to get to his feet and stagger to the dugout on the first base side. An ice bag was applied to his head.

"I wouldn't leave our third base dugout," David said. "I was too scared to come out and play once the game resumed." No one could convince him to get back on the field. So David's father, Ed, had to come down from the stands to talk with him. "David was really scared," Ed Cone recalled. "He thought he had really hurt the umpire." David's dad assured his son that the umpire knew it was an accident and that he wasn't going to hurt David because of it. "I told David that accidents happen. The umpire knew that David hadn't hit him on purpose. It was all right to go back and play the game."

But David wasn't totally convinced. He waited until the first player stepped into the batter's box before he ran back to his position. "Despite what my dad said to me, I wanted to make sure the umpire wasn't angry at me," said David.

Throughout the rest of the game, David kept a close eye on the umpire, who remained in the first base dugout with an ice bag still pressed against his forehead. "I was still scared," David said. "I thought the umpire might come across and beat me up for hitting him in the head."

The incident has remained stuck in David's mind all these years. Of course, every time he returns to his hometown of Kansas City, his old friends remind him of it. "My friends will never let me forget the day I hit the umpire with a wild throw," David said. "They'll still be telling that story when I'm 70 years old."

KELLY GRUBER

Third Baseman

Toronto Blue Jays

★ ★ ★

Kelly Gruber played baseball for the love of his grandparents Archie and Vida Hunt.

"I played every game just for them," said the Toronto Blue Jays' All-Star infielder.

Kelly grew up in Houston, Texas, and started playing organized baseball at the urging of his grandparents when he was 6 years old. They thought baseball was the finest game ever invented, and they wanted Kelly to enjoy it.

"Kelly's grandmother was a superior athlete when she was a young girl," Kelly's mother, Gloria, recalled. "But she loved baseball better than any other sport. She instilled her love for the game in Kelly."

Kelly's mom attended all his games, and so did his grandparents. If his grandparents were even a few minutes late, Kelly

would ask, "Where is Papa? Where is Mama?" Those were the pet names Kelly called his grandparents. "Kelly would be really worried until he saw them," his mother recalled. "As soon as they arrived, Kelly's face would light up and he'd be happy. He'd call out and wave to them."

Once, when Kelly was 7 years old, his grandparents were late for a game in which he was pitching. Finally, they arrived, and his grandfather walked behind the backstop to watch Kelly on the mound. Kelly was starting to deliver a pitch to the plate when he spotted his grandfather. He stopped in the middle of his motion and didn't throw the pitch. "Papa! Papa! Look at me!" Kelly called, waving his arms. "I'm pitching, Papa." The game was held up for a minute, while

Kelly talked to his grandfather from the mound. Archie just stood behind the backstop and beamed at Kelly until the umps ordered the happy, jabbering boy to start pitching again.

The umpires were never too happy to see Kelly's grandmother arrive. When Kelly pitched, Vida would spread an old lawn chair directly behind the backstop. Every time an umpire would call one of Kelly's pitches a ball, she would needle him. "Here're my glasses, ump," she would often say, taking off her glasses and waving them at the umpire. "You'd better put them on. You need them worse than I do."

There were times when Archie and Vida would do nothing but laugh at Kelly's actions—he was wild on the mound and on the base paths. Kelly could throw the ball hard, but every pitch was an adventure. There was as much chance of the ball sailing over the backstop as there was of it hitting the strike zone.

But Kelly was even wilder on the base paths. He was extremely fast, and whenever he hit the ball, he wouldn't stop running around the bases. "It was hilarious," his mother recalled. "No matter where he hit the ball, he would just keep running. He'd tap it right in front of the plate, and he'd run around first. The infielders would throw the ball to second, but Kelly would keep going until they either tagged him out or he scored. It was like a cartoon. Every time he hit the ball and it wasn't an out, he would try to score." Kelly would ignore his coaches' "stop" signs. After a while, his coaches didn't even bother to try to stop him. They knew he'd keep running. Finally, when he was 10 years old, Kelly learned to stop when he couldn't safely advance anymore.

Whether he goofed up or not on the playing field, Kelly could always count on one thing—his grandparents would always be there cheering him on. "I would look in the grandstands and see my grandparents watching me," he said. "That always comforted me."

At the beginning of each season, Kelly always gave his "Papa" a team baseball cap that Archie wore proudly to all the games.

As Kelly got older and better as a player, his grandparents dreamed of seeing him play in the major leagues. Sadly, they never did. Both died before Kelly made it to the bigs. "Although they're dead now, I still play every game just for them," said Kelly. "I know they are watching me play, and now they have the best seats in the house."

DON SLAUGHT

Catcher
Pittsburgh Pirates

★ ★ ★

In his first Little League game as a catcher, Don Slaught had a rip-roaring time—literally.

Don had to leave the field momentarily after he split his pants right up the rear from crouching a little too hard and a little too fast. Despite this embarrassing debut, Don stuck with catching to become a solid backstop with the Pittsburgh Pirates.

Don grew up across the street from the Little League field in Palos Verdes Estates, California, where he played for the Twins. Team members were issued a maroon cap and a maroon jersey, but weren't given any baseball pants. The players had to wear their own jeans.

For his first game as a Little League catcher, Don, who was 9 years old at the time, wore his oldest pair of jeans, figuring it wouldn't matter how torn up they got. "When the game was about to begin, I had to put on a big old chest protector that both teams used," Don recalled. "The catcher's mask was way too big for me, and so were the shin guards. The shin guards barely stayed on my legs."

Despite the problems with the gear, Don felt like a big shot because he was catching and he would be in the middle of all the action. As the Twins took the field in the first inning, Don swaggered out to his position behind home plate. Then he squatted to warm up his pitcher. It was then that he heard a sickening r-i-i-i-i-p!

He looked down, and his worst fears were realized. His jeans had split along the seam of his crotch. A quick check with his hands revealed that the tear had not gone up his rear end. Fortunately, the big chest protector covered the rip. "I was very embarrassed," Don recalled. "I didn't know what to do." Since he thought no one could see the tear, he figured he'd catch as though nothing had happened.

But by the time the inning was over, the rip had grown too big to hide. "When I took off the chest protector to give it to the opposing catcher, I knew everyone would see my torn pants. I had to change my pants—fast."

The good news was that he lived across the street from the ball field. The bad news was that he had to scamper past the fans to get to his house. "I ran as fast as I could back to my house and changed my pants," he said. "I returned before the inning was over, and I was ready to catch again. I never even missed a pitch."

Don might never have been a catcher had he not been so wild as a pitcher. "Don had a tremendous arm and started out as a pitcher," said his dad, John. "But he was throwing the ball everywhere but where it was supposed to go. The coaches stopped using him as a pitcher when they realized he might hurt someone. It was all for the best because now Don is a major league catcher."

PHIL BRADLEY

★ ★ ★

Phil Bradley learned a lot about baseball in college—beginning when he was 10 years old.

The future Chicago White Sox' outfielder didn't actually attend college at that young age. But he did hang around the Virginia State University baseball team when he was a youngster. In fact, he used to warm up the pitchers.

"One day, when Phil was 10 years old, he decided he could catch the team's pitchers better than the regular catchers," recalled his father, William, who coached the college team. "He went out on the field, picked up a catcher's glove, and started to warm up a pitcher. It wasn't long before the pitchers preferred to throw to him rather than throw to the regular catchers."

Phil's dad was not only the baseball coach but the school's athletic director and head of the physical education department, too. While Phil was welcome at the college practices, he wasn't allowed to do anything else on the field but catch. "Phil was always at practice, but he was strictly the warm-up catcher," his dad said. "Batting practice and fielding practice were only for the college players."

As soon as Phil saw a pitcher get up from the bench and start loosening up, he would grab a catcher's mask and glove, and rush over to catch for him. Despite his age, Phil wasn't worried about how hard those big college hurlers threw, or even about catching their breaking pitches. "Phil had a talent, and the college pitchers loved him," his father recalled. "Phil caught the ball consistently, and he gave a better target for the pitchers. They would seek him out to warm them up."

Phil did a lot more than just warm up pitchers for his father's college team. He acted as the bat boy and the assistant equipment manager. He also helped prepare the field for games and practice. And he had one more important job on the team.

"Phil's main task was to get the bubble gum," his dad said. "He had to go to the store and buy the bubble gum before games. During the game, he had to supply the players with all the bubble gum they wanted."

And while he was doing all of these things, he constantly watched the mechanics of the game. "Phil had a purpose every time he showed up at our practices," said his dad. "He wanted to learn all he could about baseball. He became a student of the game before he actually played it."

Surprisingly, Phil never caught in Little League. He was always either a pitcher or a shortstop. But his love of warming up pitchers didn't stop when his father took a new job as a professor of physical education at Western Illinois University in Macomb, Illinois.

"Phil worked as a warm-up catcher for our American Legion team," his dad said. "Even though he was 14 and too young for Legion ball, he was still part of the team. For his age, he was a terrific player. Being around all those college players sure helped him."

When he was a freshman at Macomb High School, Phil was so confident of his abilities that he decided to try out for the varsity team even though the school had never had a freshman on its team before. "I can make the team," Phil told his father. "I'm good enough to start."

His father told him to give it his best shot, and Phil did. To the surprise of many, Phil made the team as the regular second baseman. It was the start of a remarkable high school and college career. He then starred for Seattle, Philadelphia and Baltimore before joining the White Sox.

"I tried to instill in Phil from an early age that he must always strive to improve," his dad said. "If he didn't go forward, he would only slide backward. Phil always chose to go forward."

TOM GORDON

Pitcher

Kansas City Royals

★ ★ ★

Tom Gordon was such a phenomenal pitcher that he started playing against adults when he was only 13 years old—for pay!

"Tom used to disappear every Sunday," his father, Tom Sr., recalled. "A man and a boy in a pickup truck used to come by and get him. I knew he was going to play baseball, I just didn't know he was pitching for money against men's teams. I didn't discover it for three years; and when I did, I made him stop." Otherwise, Tom wouldn't have been eligible to play on the high school team.

The future Kansas City Royals hurler had already proven to his father that he could play with adults before he had reached his teens. Tom pitched for the Avon Park (Florida) Eagles, a men's league team on which his father also pitched. But Tom didn't get paid on that team.

"When Tom was 3 years old, I started working with him every day on his pitching," recalled Tom Sr. "We started out throwing fast balls. He'd pitch to me, and then I'd pitch to him. By the time he was 4, I was throwing the ball hard to him, and he was throwing hard to me."

That started a family tradition called "Burn-Out." Each would throw at the other as hard and fast as he could. Tom Sr. says they still play the game today, although Tom is now much faster than his father.

By the time Tom was 6 years old, he could throw a hard fast ball and was experimenting with a curve. Tom started throwing at a can placed beyond a 6-foot-tall fence. He'd try to curve the ball over the fence and into the can. He eventually developed such a swooping curve in high school that he could actually hurl the ball into the can.

At the age of 8, Tom was pitching and playing shortstop for the Avon Park Bagwell Lumber Little League team. "I was throwing a curve," Tom recalled. "It was just a little spinner, but no one could hit it." But his dad began to fear that Tom would hurt his arm because he was so young and didn't know how to properly throw the curve ball. "I didn't think it was a good idea for a boy to throw a curve, but Tom insisted," his dad said. "So I taught him the proper way to throw it. I hung a tire from a tree, and Tom would throw curves through it."

Tom worked hard at throwing the curve, and developed an excellent one. "Little League batters were scared of him because he threw a curve," Tom's dad said.

When Tom was 11 years old, he received a bad scare. He hurt his arm after throwing a curve ball in a Little League game. His arm hurt so much that he had to leave the mound and play second base. He fielded a grounder at that position and could only roll the ball to the first baseman. "I was very scared," Tom recalled. "When I went home, my dad wrapped my arm in hot towels. I was in severe pain that didn't go away for a while."

Tom's dad forbade him from throwing any more curve balls. It was only six months later when his dad relented and let him throw the curve again. Shortly after that, when Tom turned 12, he pitched his first real game against adults. He hurled two innings for the Eagles against Kissimmee, a nearby town. He gave up a couple of runs and struck out a batter.

Tom started pitching regularly for his dad's team when he turned 13. His dad said, "By this time, Tom could really fire a fast ball and had a great curve." He pitched very well in six games before his father started worrying that the other players were too old for Tom to hang around with. "Tom wanted to continue pitching for the Eagles," his father said. "But I was afraid the influence of grown men wasn't too good for him. I wanted him to pitch against boys his own age."

Although he stopped pitching for the Eagles, Tom started pitching secretly for pay. Every Sunday, a coach and his son would show up in a truck, and Tom would go off to play. This went on for three years, until one Sunday the coach told Tom's father, "Tom's worth every cent of the $60 I pay him to pitch." Tom's father was shocked; and he confronted Tom, who admitted that he was pitching against adults for money and didn't know there was anything wrong with that. "I ended it right there," his father said. "I wasn't going to allow Tom to hurt his future for $60 a Sunday."

Tom went on to star in high school, where he twirled three no-hitters and was named Florida State Player of the Year. His feats caught the attention of major league scouts, and soon Tom was pitching for pay again—legally.

KEVIN BASS

Outfielder

San Francisco Giants

★ ★ ★

The first time Kevin Bass tried switch-hitting, he went 7 for 7 in a Little League game and wore out the opposing team's entire pitching staff.

"But I didn't like it," recalled the San Francisco Giants' outfielder. "It felt uncomfortable, so I didn't switch-hit again until high school when I decided I wanted to be a major league ball player."

Kevin was 9 years old when his dad, Sylvester Bass, suggested that Kevin—a natural right-hander—try hitting from the left side in a game. Kevin's dad was his Little League coach and had watched the talented youngster hit left-handed in the backyard of their home in Menlo Park, California. But Kevin had never tried hitting from both sides in an actual game. He didn't need to. "Kevin hardly ever struck out as a right-hander," his dad recalled. "He was always a good hitter, even against older pitchers."

Kevin resisted his dad's advice until one Saturday afternoon when his team, the Board of Realtors, met its fiercest rival, the Kiwanis. The opponents had a roster of good right-handed pitchers who always gave Kevin the most trouble at the plate.

Kevin decided this was the game to try hitting from the opposite side; so for the first time, he went to bat as a left-hander. "It really felt awkward," Kevin recalled.

"But I hit the first pitch, and it went for a double." Encouraged by that success, Kevin tried hitting from the left side his next time up and belted a single.

The Kiwanis were caught off guard by this new switch-hitting threat. But when Kevin came to bat the third time, the Kiwanis' coach was ready for him. The coach put in a new pitcher, an ace lefty. "When I saw that," recalled Kevin, "I asked the umpire if it was okay if I switched and hit right-handed. I thought I had to have his permission."

Hitting from his familiar, right-handed stance, Kevin faced the challenge. He smacked a home run! Kevin batted four more times during the game. Every time the Kiwanis switched pitchers, Kevin hit from the opposite side and rapped another hit. The Kiwanis used their entire staff of five pitchers trying to stop Kevin's hitting barrage. But none of them could get him out. He led his team to a 14-1 slaughter with a homer, three doubles, and three singles.

"Going 7 for 7 surprised me more than it did everybody else," Kevin said. "But I still didn't like switch-hitting, so I quit doing it after that game."

Despite the pleas of his teammates, Kevin didn't switch-hit again until he was in high school. By then, he realized that switch-hitting would improve his chances of making it to the major leagues. "When I reached high school, I wanted to be a power hitter," said Kevin. "But then my dad reminded me of the time I went 7 for 7. He said I would be more valuable to a major league team if I could hit to all fields as a switch-hitter. He had been right when I was in Little League, and this time I was smart enough to follow his advice. I'm glad I did."

TERRY PENDLETON

In his first year in Little League, Terry Pendleton was such a weak batter that he got only one hit all season. He walked twice and struck out every other time in the twenty games that he played.

But he didn't give up. He spent the entire winter learning how to hit. The following year, Terry became such an impressive batter that he made the all-star team.

The future St. Louis Cardinals' infielder was 9 years old when he joined the Oxnard (California) Cubs. He started the season as a part-time right fielder. "They stuck the worst player in right field," Terry recalled. "That was me. I was the worst player on the team."

Although the coach put him in right field in the last two innings of each game, it was not because Terry couldn't field. He was a good glove man and had a fine arm.

His problem was at the plate. "Terry would get his swings," his dad, Alfred, recalled. "He just couldn't hit the ball. He especially had a problem with high pitches. He'd always swing at them, even if they were over his head."

Terry's one hit all year was a cheap fluke. He swatted at a high pitch and popped it up behind the second baseman for a single. "The second baseman misplayed the ball," Terry's father said with a laugh. "He should've caught it, but he misjudged it. Terry was so happy that he had hit the ball and made it to first that no one had the heart to tell him the ball should have been caught."

His inability to hit discouraged Terry at first. "I thought about quitting after every game," he admitted, "but my parents would talk me out of it and tell me that I would get better. They said to go out and have fun." But Terry felt that the only reason he was on the team at all was because his godfather, Wallace Anger, was the coach. Although Terry felt embarrassed, he took his parents' advice and continued to play.

Terry gained loads of confidence in mid-season when he was made a surprise starter. Coach Anger was sick for a game, so the assistant coach made out the lineup and started Terry at shortstop. "It amazed everyone since Terry had no experience and had only been used at the end of games in right field," his father said. "But the assistant coach must have seen something good in Terry, and he was proven right."

Terry was brilliant at short, stopping everything hit his way. On one play, he brought the crowd to its feet by racing into the hole, backhanding a hard grounder, and throwing the runner out at first. Terry then became the Cubs' regular shortstop. "From that moment on, he started feeling better about the game," his dad recalled. "He was determined that if he couldn't get a hit, he wouldn't allow anyone on the other team to have one, either."

But Terry wasn't satisfied with just being a good fielder. He wanted to be a good hitter, too. When the baseball season ended and his teammates were playing Pop Warner Football, Terry was hitting baseballs. "I skipped every other sport to concentrate on baseball," Terry said. "I worked very hard that winter to become a hitter."

Terry's dad and coaches went with Terry to a nearby park, where they took turns pitching batting practice to him and giving him pointers on hitting. Eventually, Terry started feeling comfortable in the batter's box and was belting pitches to all fields.

"The following season, Terry started hitting right away," his dad said. "It settled him down completely." That year, Terry was named shortstop of the all-star team. The Cubs' weakest hitter the year before was now one of the league's most feared batters. Even his fine fielding improved. "I learned the value of hard work," Terry said. "It made me a good player, and I still work hard today to become even better."

LEE GUETTERMAN

Twelve-year-old Lee Guetterman was psyched. He had just been picked as the starting pitcher in his first all-star game, and he was raring to go. But then, on the day before the big game, he tried to loosen his arm by rubbing it with heating balm. Instead, his arm went numb. And the game turned into a nightmare for Lee.

The future New York Yankees relief pitcher was a member of the Gators Little League team in National City, California, when he was chosen to the all-star team. He was thrilled because it was the first time he had been selected for the team. When his all-star team coach learned that Lee had never done anything to loosen his pitching arm before games, he told Lee to take two aspirins and rub his arm with heating balm. It would make him pitch better, said the coach. So Lee did what the coach told him.

But when Lee took the mound the next day, he discovered to his horror that he had no feeling in his pitching arm because the muscles were too relaxed from the balm.

"When a coach tells you to do something as a Little Leaguer, you think he knows what he's talking about," Lee said. "I learned that wasn't true. My coach's advice hurt me. I had no strength at all in my arm. I couldn't really pitch because I couldn't feel my arm. I didn't have anything on the ball, and I got clobbered." Lee lasted only three innings, and his team lost 8-1.

But he learned a valuable lesson. "I learned to prepare for a game the way I know best," he said. "Coaches aren't always right. You have to discover for yourself what is right or wrong for you. You should try things in practice before you try them in a game."

The loss was a big disappointment to Lee, who had finally realized his dream of being an all-star. Three years earlier, Lee didn't have that dream. In fact, he almost quit baseball because he thought he was an awful player.

Lee started playing organized baseball when he was 9 years old. He wasn't very good then and played briefly in only six games. The next year, in National City, Lee got to play in every game because that was a league rule. But he never started, and collected only five hits all year.

The following year, when he was 11 years old and being driven to the season's first day of practice, he told his dad, "I don't want to play baseball anymore."

"Why?" asked his dad, Art, a Navy chaplain. "You love the game."

"I'm not any good at baseball," Lee replied. "I didn't get to play very much at all last year. I won't get to play again this year."

Art Guetterman knew his son hadn't played much because he hadn't developed as much physically as the other boys. But over the past year, Lee had grown stronger and had gained more experience. His dad had to find a way to convince Lee that he faced a bright future on the team.

"When we got to the field, I asked Lee to wait on one side of the snack shack," his father recalled. "I wanted him out of sight but within earshot as I talked to his coach."

Lee's dad asked the coach what he thought Lee's prospects were for the coming year. The coach told him that he expected Lee to be the team's top relief pitcher.

"Is Lee a good ballplayer?" his dad asked. "Was he good last year?"

"He was very good for his age," the coach replied. "I expect he'll even be better this year."

Lee's dad thanked the coach, then turned to Lee and said, "Would you play this year, son—for me?"

Lee, having overheard the encouraging words of his coach, readily agreed. He started to feel more confident as the year went on; and by the time he was 12, he dreamed of being not only a Little League all-star but also a major league pitcher someday.

Both his dreams came true.

KEN GRIFFEY JR.

Ken Griffey Jr. was such a gifted player in his first year in Cincinnati's Knothole League that he never made an out as a batter and never lost a game as a pitcher.

He knew how to hit—his batting average was a perfect 1.000—and he knew how to pitch—he won all twelve of his games. What he didn't know was how to handle the small failures every player experiences in baseball.

Not until his first at-bat the following year did Ken, then 11 years old, make his first Knothole League out. He was heartsick and sobbed all the way back to the bench. The future Seattle Mariners' All-Star outfielder and 1989 American League Rookie of the Year just didn't understand how anyone could get him out. In fact, he was so crushed that his mother, Birdie, had to come down out of the stands and console him on the bench.

"Look at your dad," she said, referring to his father, Ken Sr., then a major league All-Star for the world champion Cincinnati Reds. "Your dad makes outs all the time, and he's a big leaguer."

Ken looked at his mom through his tears and mumbled, "That's him, not me. I don't make outs." Ken didn't play the rest of the game. He just couldn't go out on the field because he was so upset.

Eventually, Ken learned to accept a fact of baseball life—you can't get a hit with every at-bat. Ken also learned another tough lesson—how to handle abusive fans. Unfortunately, there were many adults who always heckled Ken simply because he was the son of a major leaguer.

"The little league fans were very abusive to Kenny," his mother said. "They would yell things at him, like his father was a lousy player. As the wife of a major leaguer, I've heard many bad things said about my husband. But I learned to take it. I told Kenny that he'd have to take it, too."

Ken didn't let the harassment bother him because he was supremely confident as a young baseball player. In fact, he loved nothing better than to silence the loudmouths with his batting and pitching skills. Once during a game, the opposing pitcher's mother was yelling nasty things to Ken. When Ken stepped into the batter's box, she yelled to the pitcher, "Strike him out, son. He's not his dad. He can't hit at all."

Ken called time, turned to the woman in the stands, and asked her, "Why are you telling your son that lie, lady?"

Ken stepped back in, and on the next pitch, he walloped a mammoth home run. When he crossed home plate, he just smiled at the now-silent mother. When the ball was retrieved, his coach gave it to Ken as a memento of that sweet revenge.

Another time, in the last inning of a game that Ken was pitching, the fans were heckling him. The opposing coach tried to rattle Ken by ordering his batters to step out of the batter's box after each pitch and take their time getting back in. The umpire told Ken to pitch even if the batters weren't in the batter's box. That started even more badgering of Ken from the fans.

Finally, his mother erupted for the first and only time at a little league game. "Kenny," she yelled from the stands. "Would you please strike out these last three batters so we can shut these people up?"

Ken grinned at his mother and shouted back, "Okay, Mom!" Nine pitches later the side was retired and Ken's team had won. After the game, the umpire came over to Birdie and thanked her for speaking up.

One of the best lessons that Birdie taught her son was that no matter how good he was, he was still only one member of a team. Birdie insisted that Ken's coaches treat him exactly like every other player and make him follow the same rules. "Because my mother insisted that I be treated like everyone else, I developed the true spirit of baseball," Ken said. "Baseball is a team game; and while you may be the star of your team, it doesn't matter how good you are if your team loses. It takes a team effort to win. It's something I've never forgotten."

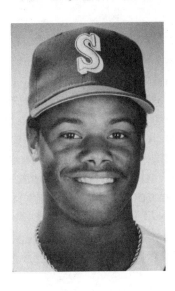

KEN CAMINITI

Ken Caminiti hated to bat when he was a Little Leaguer because he was afraid of being hit with the baseball.

The future Houston Astros' infielder didn't have any problems when he started playing at the age of 7 since the league used a pitching machine. But when he turned 10 and had to face real pitchers, Ken was stricken with fear.

"I always batted with one foot 'in the bucket' "—his lead foot would move away from the plate—"because I was so scared of being hit," Ken recalled. "I didn't even like baseball because of my fear. I only played because my parents wanted me to play."

At the age of 7, Ken was the youngest member of his team when he started play-ing shortstop in the San Jose (California) Union Little League. At first, he wasn't afraid to bat. "Everyone batted against a pitching machine," Ken recalled. "There was no chance of being hit by a pitch."

Ken never had any problems in the field, even at this young age. His fielding was superb as a 10-year-old. But his perspective on baseball changed then. "I started facing real pitchers," Ken recalled. "I didn't like it one bit. I would've quit except my dad kept me going. He kept telling me to hang in there."

Part of the reason Ken continued to play was that his mother, Yvonne, bribed him with an ice-cream sundae for every hit he got. "He loved getting the ice cream," Ken's dad, Lee, recalled. "He started hitting the ball better after his mother offered him that bribe."

Still, Ken was afraid of being hit by a pitched ball. Batting practice wasn't too bad because someone's father always pitched, and Ken knew he wasn't going to be hit. But games were a nightmare for Ken because he kept getting plunked with pitches.

"Whenever I got hit by a pitch, I would cry all the way to first base," Ken recalled. "It was that bad for me. I don't know which was worse—the fear or the pain."

Once, when he was 11 years old, Ken was hit in the back with a pitch. His father was coaching third base at the time. As Ken started for first base with tears rolling down his cheeks, his father walked over and said, "It doesn't hurt that bad, does it?"

"Yes, it does," Ken replied. "I don't want to play anymore. I don't like being hit."

His father rubbed his back and talked Ken into continuing. "I tried to put everything into perspective for Ken," his dad recalled. "I tried to tell him the pitch really wasn't thrown that fast. But to him at his young age, the pitchers were throwing bullets. He still hated to bat."

It wasn't until Ken was in high school that he finally kicked his fear of being hit with a pitch. By this time, Ken had developed into a solid line drive hitter even though he was still afraid to go to the plate. "Finally, I had to come to terms with my fear," Ken said. "I had to decide whether I was going to be afraid all of my life, or just bear down and take it."

Ken sat down and thought about it. He decided that he wasn't going to let fear rule his life. "I just decided it was time to be a man," Ken said. "I wanted to play baseball, so I had to get over being scared at the plate. I started going up and forgetting that there was a chance I could get hit. After a while, my fear went away completely, and I started to enjoy playing baseball more than I ever did before. I conquered my fear, and it made me happier."

TOM BRUNANSKY

Outfielder
___
Boston
Red Sox

★ ★ ★

Every time young Tom Brunansky made a big play on the baseball diamond, he would hear loud, happy honking coming from his father's car parked on a hill above the field.

The future Boston Red Sox home run slugger would turn and grin at his father, Joe, who watched all of Tom's games in his car on a hill about 200 feet from the right field fence of the San Jose Little League field in West Covina, California. "Every time I hit a home run, my dad would blow the car horn," Tom recalled. "If I made a good play in the field, he'd blow the horn, too."

While Tom's mom, Rae, sat in the grandstands at every game, his dad could never watch a game from there because he got too upset if things weren't going right on the baseball field. "I had a habit of saying things first and thinking about them later," Tom's dad admitted. "If I sat in my car, I could yell and say anything I wanted without bothering other people. I didn't want people thinking badly of Tom because of something I might say in the heat of a game. I particularly didn't want to get on Tom if he did something wrong."

Joe resorted to cheering from his car after behaving somewhat badly while sitting in the grandstands watching Tom's older brother, Joe Jr., play ball. Sometimes Joe Sr. would lose his temper with umpires or even with the young players when they botched a play. "I just got too excited at baseball games," said Joe Sr. "In the heat of battle, I became so wrapped up in the game that I hollered things that I regretted later."

Tom understood his dad's feelings and didn't mind at all when his dad decided to watch him play from the car. "When I went out to my position, I'd look up on the hill, and there would be my dad's car," Tom said. "I'd give him a little smile and a wave. When I did something really good and my dad would honk the horn, I'd always smile up at the car. I was just glad my dad was there."

Tom played the outfield, pitched, and played first base for the Tigers, his Little League team. His dad had plenty of opportunities to honk the horn since Tom was one of the stars of the team. In fact, the league president lost plenty of money because Tom was such a great player. "The president promised Tom a hamburger, french fries, and a milk shake from the field's snack shack every time he hit a home run," Joe Sr. recalled. "Tom was hitting so many home runs that the league president was keeping the shack in business. Tom wanted that food!"

Tom was a long ball hitter from the time he started in Little League at the age of 8. When he was 9, he belted one of the longest home runs ever hit at the Little League field. "It was an awesome blast," his father recalled. "No one could believe a young boy could hit a baseball that far. It went well over 300 feet."

Tom loved the game of baseball from the start; and the first time he made the team and was given a baseball uniform, he was thrilled. He ran up to his father and shouted, "Look, Dad! I have a real baseball uniform!" Tom was standing proudly in a uniform that was too big for him. Nothing fit at all. The hat was too big, and the sleeves and pant legs were too long. But Tom didn't care.

"It's something I'll never forget," Tom's dad said. "Even today, when Tom takes the field in his major league uniform, I still see that little boy in the oversized uniform jumping up and down with joy over wearing his first uniform. Tom will always be that little boy to me."

Today, Tom's dad watches his son play from the grandstands or on TV, but they both remember the days when Joe Sr. sat in the car high above the field. "I always listened for the car horn," Tom said. "I knew it was my dad's way of giving me a pat on the back."

TED POWER

Pitcher

Pittsburgh Pirates

★ ★ ★

Something was wrong with Ted Power.

Normally, the 7-year-old pitcher had exceptional control for his age. The future Pittsburgh Pirates' reliever almost always was in total command on the mound whenever he pitched for his little league team in Guthrie, Oklahoma.

But on this day, something was bothering him. In the second inning, he had lost his control and walked six batters. When he did get the ball over the plate, it wasn't as fast as he normally threw it, and the batters were banging out hits. In between pitches, Ted fidgeted, crossed and uncrossed his legs, squirmed, and bit his lip.

On the bench, his dad, Ray, who was the assistant coach, turned to head coach Harold Carey and said, "I can't figure out what's wrong with Ted. It's not like him."

"Maybe we ought to bring Luther in," said Harold, referring to the team's other pitcher.

Just then, Ted's mother, Theda, walked from the stands to the bench and told the coaches, "I know what's wrong with Ted. He has to go to the bathroom!"

Harold immediately called time out and jogged to the mound. He discovered that Ted's mom knew her son well. Ted indeed had to pee. In fact, he had to pee real bad. But he was just too embarrassed to tell anyone.

Unfortunately for Ted, they were playing the game on the ball field of an elementary school that had all its doors locked.

There were no other bathrooms nearby. And the area around the trees behind the backstop was occupied with parents and kids. Harold squinted beyond the outfield and noticed there were some big trees about a block away. Turning to the umpire, the coach said, "Ump, we need a minute or two to take care of a slight emergency. The boy has to go real bad."

The ump nodded. Then Harold pointed to the trees in the distance and told Ted, "Run to those trees over there and take your leak, and then hustle right back." Ted scampered as best he could with a full bladder and found a big tree. Out of sight of the crowd, he relieved himself and then raced back to the mound.

"I remember that the kids on the field didn't quite know what was going on, but the adults caught on right away," recalled Ted's dad. "There were a few chuckles. When Ted returned to the mound, he was a different pitcher. All of a sudden, he was throwing hard and throwing strikes. They didn't score a run off of him after that."

The Power family still laughs about that game—and about a rather painful batting practice that happened the same year. "I used to take Ted to a field near our house and pitch to him while his older sister, Susie, would field the balls," recalled Ted's dad. "One day, I was a little wild. I hit him in the knee and then in the side, and finally I accidentally clipped him in the ear—and he didn't have on a batting helmet. Ted yelled in pain and told me he'd never let me pitch to him again. I hit him more than he hit the ball that day. Maybe that's what has made him so tough."

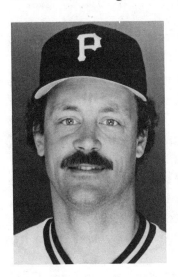

CHRIS SABO

Third Baseman
—
Cincinnati Reds

★ ★ ★

Chris Sabo couldn't get enough baseball. In fact, when he wasn't playing second base as a teenager, he was umpiring league games. But he quickly discovered that calling a player out was a lot tougher than getting him out.

"I couldn't believe the abuse an umpire takes," recalled the Cincinnati Reds' All-Star third baseman. "It was unbelievable the things that parents, players, and fans would say to me as an umpire. As a player, I promised myself that I would never get angry with an umpire again."

Chris started playing baseball in his native Detroit when he was 7 years old. He learned to hit with an old wooden stick. First, he painted the handle orange to simulate the pine tar that was used on the bat of his favorite player, Detroit Tigers star Norm Cash. Chris then tossed stones from his mom's garden up in the air and swatted them with his makeshift bat toward the neighbor's house.

"Chris had ruined the aluminum siding on our neighbor's house," his mother, Sandy, recalled. "The whole side of the house was dented from the stones that Chris had hit. He completely cleared the stones out of my garden by the time he was 9."

Chris and his family moved to Farmington, Michigan, where Chris became an all-star second baseman and the top hitter on his Little League team. Chris loved baseball so much that he wanted to be on the diamond even when he wasn't playing. So at the age of 14, Chris decided to become an umpire. "Chris went to umpiring school for three weeks," his mother recalled. "When he graduated, he started umpiring T-ball, and eventually umpired games all over town for other leagues."

As an umpire, Chris learned to be authoritative and to make his calls loudly and clearly. "If someone came rushing at me, I had to stand my ground," Chris said. "An umpire has to control the game."

But sometimes he became a little too intimidating with the young players even though he didn't mean to be. In one T-ball game, a young batter swung three times and missed the ball. "You're out!" Chris shouted a bit too loudly. The little boy dropped to the ground as if he had been shot. Everyone rushed to see if he was hurt. He wasn't. Lying on the ground crying, the boy pointed at Chris and sobbed, "He said I was out. I've been kicked out of the game." Chris had been so vigorous in making the call that he scared the boy into thinking he had been ejected from the game. Chris apologized and explained to the boy the meaning of being called "out."

After Chris had gained some umpiring experience, he moved on to umpiring girls' softball games and also older boys' games. He even umpired in the same league in which he played. "Chris played twice a week and practiced at least two more times a week," his mother recalled. "Then he would umpire about four games a week, sometimes two a day."

He particularly liked umpiring the games of the 16-and-older girls' softball league so he could spend time with the pretty girls. But he didn't like umpiring games in which his younger sister, Beth, played. He once called her out on a third strike. "Beth yelled at him and wouldn't speak to him for a week," Chris's mom recalled. "He learned not to umpire another one of her games."

But Chris's biggest lessons were learned from the fans and parents. "Chris would come home very upset after umpiring games," his mother said. "He couldn't believe the things adults would yell at him from the stands. Thirty-year-old men would rush him and threaten to punch him in the face whenever he made a call they didn't like."

It deeply affected Chris, who finally told his mother, "I don't want to be an umpire anymore. I can't believe the abuse they take. It isn't worth it."

Today, as a major leaguer, Chris occasionally has his arguments with umpires over what he thinks are bad calls. "I sometimes get angry at an umpire's call," Chris said. "But I feel sorry right away. I can't help remembering what it was like for me to be an umpire."

BRET SABERHAGEN

Pitcher
—
Kansas
City
Royals

★ ★ ★

Nine-year-old Bret Saberhagen thought he was too good to practice before his first Little League tryout. He quickly found out how wrong he was. In the field, Bret muffed everything hit his way; and at the plate, he couldn't hit the ball out of the infield. In fact, he was so bad that he was the next-to-last player drafted in the league.

"I had been a star in T-ball," recalled the Kansas City Royals' two-time Cy Young award-winning pitcher. "I figured I'd be a star in Little League. So I didn't practice, and I paid the price."

In T-ball the year before, Bret was a super player who seemed to be a natural-born fielder. Bret roamed the field, trying to play everyone's position for his team in the Northridge (California) T-ball League. "Bret caught everything anyone hit," his father, Bob, recalled. "He was a real go-getter. We had to beg him to give the other kids a chance to field. Bret could also hit. He really crushed the ball off the tee. He looked like he didn't belong with the other kids. He was just so much better."

His performance in T-ball made Bret overconfident. He wasn't concerned about facing next season's tryouts for the Van Nuys-Reseda Little League. The tryouts were used to determine how good a player was. The coaches in the league took turns drafting the best players first and then worked down the draft list until all the players were picked. This way, the draft evened out the competition.

In the weeks prior to the draft, Bret didn't play any baseball other than tossing the ball around with friends. "Bret wasn't really practicing or working out," his father said. "He was just fooling around and having fun."

Bret's mother, Linda, kept urging him to practice before he went to the tryouts.

"I don't need to practice," Bret replied. "I don't want to do it. I'm good enough to make it."

On the way to the tryout, Bret was supremely confident and expected to be the first player chosen in the draft. He figured he would do great in the tryout. He was shocked to learn differently.

"Bret humiliated himself in the tryout," his dad recalled. "He muffed everything hit to him. He couldn't field anything. And he couldn't hit at all. He just did everything wrong. Bret put on the most awful display of baseball you ever saw. He humiliated himself into tears."

Bret's performance led to further embarrassment. He was drafted next to last. "He would've been drafted last except two coaches flipped a coin to see who would get Bret and the other player," Bret's dad recalled. "The coach who got Bret thought he had gotten the worst player in the draft."

Bret learned from his mistake, though. On the way home, he told his dad, "I should have practiced. I'll never be unprepared again."

From that day forth, Bret turned into a hard worker and saw the value of practice. In fact, he practiced longer and harder than any of his teammates and totally surprised his Little League coach, Mike Morris. The coach soon realized that he had lucked out—he had acquired the best player in the league.

"It was a shock to find out," Morris told Bret's father, "that the last boy I picked in the draft turned out to be the best player I ever saw."

DAVE MAGADAN

First
Baseman

New York
Mets

★ ★ ★

Like many Little Leaguers, Dave Magadan dreamed of breaking batting records. Unfortunately, the things he broke most often playing baseball were windows.

"Between Dave and his brother, Joe, there were quite a few windows broken," recalled his father, Joe Sr. "I'd fix them and they'd break them."

The New York Mets' hard-hitting first baseman grew up in Tampa, Florida. He first started learning how to hit by playing ball with Joe Jr., who was four years older, in a vacant lot behind their house. They took turns pitching hardballs to each other and hitting toward their house, about 150 feet away. And that caused problems.

"My husband and I would be sitting quietly at home and suddenly there would be the crash of another broken window," said Dave's mom, Alice. "They broke so many windows that it seemed we were always cleaning up broken glass. Sometimes when it happened, I tried to hide it from their father.

"One time Dave broke the bathroom window, and I didn't want my husband to find out because he would have been furious. Dave's dad had just fixed the window the day before when Dave broke it with a baseball."

Mrs. Magadan put a large plant on the window sill to hide the hole in the glass, and pulled the venetian blinds down, hoping her husband wouldn't raise them and see the hole. The next day, she asked a neighbor to fix the window and begged him to keep it all hush-hush.

"Usually, the boys would break the window in the bathroom," recalled their father. "But sometimes, they hit the window in the bedroom. At the time, I might have gotten a little angry with them, but not for long."

Dave's mom always knew what to say to calm their father. "I would just laugh it off and tell Joe Sr. that we should be glad our boys could hit so well."

Despite the broken windows, Joe Sr. was proud of his sons and how well they could hit the ball because he was instrumental in teaching them how to hit. Joe Sr. coached Joe Jr.'s Little League team and always took time out from practice to work on Dave's hitting. "I started pitching to Dave when he was 3 1/2 years old," said Joe Sr. "He was a natural hitter. Soon I was throwing as hard to him as I was to the older boys on the team.

"Dave batted right-handed and hit with power. But he also swung and missed a lot of pitches. However, when he batted left-handed, he always seemed to connect. He could spray line drives to all fields. So I told him to hit only left-handed because he would be more valuable to his team." Today, in the major leagues, Dave still bats left-handed even though he is a natural right-hander.

Dave also got some help with his hitting from his famous cousin and godfather, Lou Piniella, who broke into the majors with the Kansas City Athletics when Dave was 7. Lou, an All-Star who played for eighteen years in the bigs and now manages the Cincinnati Reds, used to come over to the Magadan house and give Dave and his brother pointers on the fine art of hitting.

"Every year, Dave kept improving as a hitter," said his dad. "He was an eager learner. He just loved to bat. But when he and Joe played in the back, there was always the chance that one of our windows would get hit.

"I even started using a screen to cover the bathroom window and protect it from flying baseballs. But usually the boys or I would forget to put it up. There's still a crack in the window from the last time Dave hit it. The window didn't break because the ball hit the frame. I've thought about fixing it; but now that Dave's in the major leagues, maybe I'll just leave it as a reminder of how well he could hit when he was a boy."

Catcher

**San
Francisco
Giants**

★ ★ ★

Terry Kennedy lived a childhood Little Leaguers only dream about. He got to hang around with baseball super stars. Terry played catch with Catfish Hunter, took batting practice with Reggie Jackson, and shagged fly balls with Billy Williams.

"To me, they were just guys who worked for my dad," recalled the San Francisco Giants' veteran All-Star catcher. His dad is Bob Kennedy, a former major leaguer from 1939 to 1957, who later managed the Chicago Cubs (1963-65) and the Oakland Athletics (1968).

His dad often took him to the clubhouse and introduced him to the players. "I met players like Mickey Mantle, Roger Maris, Brooks Robinson, Carl Yastrzemski, and Ernie Banks," recalled Terry. "I never realized some of those guys I hung around with were future Hall-of-Famers."

Between the ages of 7 and 9 when Terry lived in Chicago, he began receiving baseball tips from the Cubs. "My best friend back then was [Cubs outfielder] Billy Williams," said Terry. "He talked to me a lot about playing in the big leagues. I got some of my best batting tips from Billy."

Other great players contributed to Terry's baseball education. When his dad coached in Atlanta in 1967, home run slugger Hank Aaron took Terry under his wing. Even while Aaron was closing in on Babe Ruth's home run record, he spent time with Terry, showing him how to pick the right pitch to hit and how to swing for power.

The next year, when Terry's dad became manager of the Oakland Athletics, super star Reggie Jackson gave Terry some hitting advice. But despite the attention he received from baseball's top stars, Terry didn't display any real talent as a player at first.

"I played in Little League just one year when I was 12 years old," said Terry. "I wasn't very good. Mostly, I sat on the bench, and I didn't get many at-bats. I was scared of the pitchers and just didn't get much out of the experience. I guess I hadn't paid attention to all the advice I'd been getting from my big league friends."

Because he had been exposed to so many major leaguers while he was grow-ing up, Terry didn't know that he was living a life that most other kids envied. It wasn't until he was 11 years old that he understood just how lucky he was. "I first realized what great people those players were when my dad was coaching the Braves," he said. "It was the last day of the season, and I went through the Atlanta clubhouse crying my eyes out because we were all saying good-bye. I still miss those guys and all the things they taught me."

By the time he reached high school, Terry made a personal commitment to become the best ballplayer possible. "I got a late start, but then all that valuable coaching from those All-Stars and Hall-of-Famers began to sink in," he said. "I began to put into practice everything that I had learned."

Terry said he has one regret. "I hadn't asked any of them for their autographs, and I wish I had," he said. "I could have had the greatest autograph collection of all time."

TERRY PUHL

Outfielder

Houston Astros

★ ★ ★

Terry Puhl didn't know much about baseball other than the fact that it was an American game. Besides, there weren't any ball diamonds way out on the plains of Saskatchewan, Canada, where he grew up.

But then in 1969, when Terry was 12 years old, the Montreal Expos became a National League team. Suddenly, Canadian kids like Terry had a batch of heroes other than hockey players.

"When the Expos came along, it was really a big deal," the Houston Astros' outfielder recalled. "Where I grew up, no one knew anything about baseball, but then everybody wanted to learn how to play.

"Baseball became an alternative to hockey. We were sure the Expos would send scouts around to find Canadian kids, and we wanted to show them what we had. Unfortunately, what we had wasn't much. We didn't even know how to play."

Terry and his friends knew how to throw a ball and hold a bat, but they had to learn baseball fundamentals on their own—like how to bunt, how to field grounders, and how to run the bases. "We didn't know any of the basics that American kids learn during their first year in Little League," said Terry. "And we didn't have anyone to teach us. We just played ball and never knew if we were doing things right or wrong."

The baseball bug bit Terry harder than

his friends. Even though he lived in Melville, Saskatchewan—3,000 miles away from the Expos—he dreamed of the day when he would play in the major leagues. But he had a lot to overcome.

With the long Canadian winters, the baseball season was only two months long. And even during the short season, there weren't any nice diamonds on which to play. "Mostly we just played in open fields," Terry said. "We'd go out somewhere, throw down some kind of bags for the bases, and that would be our baseball diamond."

One such field was the site of the "Gopher Game" during Terry's first year of playing baseball. In a game with his pals, Terry played right field. Since the pitchers couldn't pitch and the hitters couldn't hit, there wasn't much action to follow. Even for Terry, the game was boring.

To keep busy, he picked up some rocks and practiced throwing. Suddenly, he spied a target. A gopher that lived in right field had poked its head out of its hole. Terry was not cruel to animals, but he started throwing the rocks at the gopher just to make it duck. Terry's aim was better than he realized. "In between innings, I returned to the bench swinging this dead gopher by the tail," Terry recalled. "That was my first baseball trophy."

But it wasn't his last. After the "Gopher Game," Terry worked hard to develop his baseball skills. Other little league teams began to form as Canadian baseball fever spread. But the kids from Melville had to travel great distances to games. Terry's dad would pack the boys in an old army bus and drive 100 miles or more to Moose Jaw or Saskatoon to play other little league teams.

When Terry was 14, the Melville team won thirty-eight games without a defeat—and he pitched thirty of those games. At the age of 17, Terry played on a team that won the Canadian national championship. That same year, his dream came closer to reality. The Canadian kid who didn't play baseball until he was 12 years old signed his first major league contract.

KEVIN GROSS

When Kevin Gross was 12 years old, he was the thinnest and smallest player on the Diamond Bar (California) All-Stars. Yet opposing coaches in the all-star tournament tried to stop him from playing—because he was too good!

"Although I didn't look like a power pitcher, I really had a good fast ball for my age," recalled Kevin. "I also had very good control."

The future Montreal Expos' pitcher was an overpowering strikeout king in Little League. Opposing coaches just couldn't believe a 12-year-old could be so dominant on the mound. They were convinced he was older than he really was. For the tournament, Kevin was ordered to produce his birth certificate to prove his age. He did, but that still didn't satisfy some of the coaches.

"One coach said that something was wrong even though Kevin's birth certificate said he was the right age," Kevin's mom, Margot, recalled. "He raised heck because he didn't think Kevin should be allowed to pitch. And the reason was that Kevin threw too fast! Another coach said it was unfair to make anyone hit against Kevin. He insisted there was something fishy going on. He believed there had to be some illegal reason why Kevin could pitch as well as he did."

Tournament officials disallowed the protests and let Kevin pitch. He quickly showed why the opposing coaches didn't want him to play.

"In the first game I pitched in the tournament, I threw a no-hit perfect game," said Kevin. "No one could touch me." The six-inning masterpiece came against the Pomona American All-Stars. Kevin mowed down Pomona, striking out fourteen of the eighteen batters he faced. He also hit two home runs in the game.

After the game, several opposing coaches again lodged a protest. But their complaints were brushed aside by tourney officials. "How could you penalize a player for being too good?" Kevin's mom said. "That's what the opposing coaches were trying to do."

A week later, Kevin took the mound again in the tournament. This time, he faced San Dimas in the area semifinals. Kevin was overpowering again. "I had complete control of the game," he recalled. "I went into the sixth inning with another no-hitter."

Kevin hadn't been quite so perfect in this game. He had walked two batters, but he left them stranded. In the final inning, Kevin struck out the lead-off hitter. The next boy hit a pop-up for the second out. Kevin was now within one out of pitching back-to-back no-hitters. "The third batter was a weak hitter," Kevin recalled. "I thought I had a second no-hitter for sure." But the batter, Alan Quay, hit a slow bouncer toward short and beat it out for an infield hit. Kevin blew away the next batter on three pitches for his ninth strikeout of the game and settled for a one-hit, 12-0 victory.

As a release from the tensions of baseball, Kevin took up oil painting. He painted outdoor scenes and animals, an activity that helped him cope with the pressures of being one of the area's best Little League pitchers.

"Painting cushioned my troubles growing up," Kevin said. "It relaxed me before and after games. I'd come home after a game and immediately start painting. I still do that today."

Kevin lived, ate, and slept baseball. He always knew that he wanted to be a major leaguer. "Mama, I'm going to be a big baseball man," Kevin repeatedly told his mother when he first started playing the game. "I'm going to play in the big leagues." By the time Kevin hurled his first no-hitter, no one doubted his words for a minute.

DON MATTINGLY

<table>
<tr><td>

**First
Baseman**
___

**New York
Yankees**

★ ★ ★

</td><td>

</td></tr>
</table>

It was as though Don Mattingly was a genie who could grant his friends' wishes.

During one memorable game, every time he heard family friends yell for him to hit a home run, he belted one—and in the exact spot where they had wanted him to hit it!

The New York Yankees' super star played first base for Great Scott Grocery in Evansville, Indiana, where he grew up. He had had some great games, but nothing like his three-homer day when he was 10.

In the first inning at Northside Little League Park, Don stepped into the batter's box, tugged at his wine-colored cap, and adjusted his pinstriped jersey. Suddenly, he heard friendly voices from behind the chain link outfield fence shouting, "C'mon, Donny! Hit it out here to left field!"

He smiled as he recognized his parents, William and Mary, and some family friends. No one really expected him to whack a homer because, although he usually made contact, he was never considered a slugger. Yet Don walloped the first pitch right where they had asked—over the left field fence!

"He was so happy that he gave out an Indian war whoop as he rounded the bases," recalled his mother. "Our friends got such a kick out of it that the next time he came up to bat, they yelled, 'Let's see you hit one over the center field fence!' Sure enough, Don knocked the ball right over the center field fence—and that was about 185 feet away. Boy, did he give a happy holler when he ran around the bases."

In Don's third and final time at bat, the family friends shouted to him, "Okay, Donny, now hit one over the right field fence!" Incredibly, Don did just that—he smacked a drive that cleared the right field fence. It was an astounding performance.

By the end of the game, Don had blasted one round-tripper to each field, just as his friends had asked. Never before or since in Little League had he ever swatted three homers in a game. But on this day, Don looked like a slugger.

Interestingly enough, that's not the game Don remembers most about that Little League year. In fact, the game that still sticks in his mind was a low point for him. "It was the first game of the season," he recalled. "I struck out three straight times against the same pitcher. I was so upset that I cried after the game. I was hurt and embarrassed."

Don was such a good hitter in Little League that he had never struck out three times in a game before. So when it happened to him, he was shocked. "Striking out hurt him more than anything," said his dad. "I told him not to worry about it. I told Don, 'Go out and have a good time, and do the best you can. If things don't work out, forget about it.' "

But whiffing three straight times spurred Don to try even harder. He promised himself that he would never let it happen again. "I told myself that it was just one game and that there's always tomorrow," said Don. "I learned that failure is part of the game. You don't go out there to fail, but it will happen from time to time. It's impor-

tant to learn from your mistakes in order to be the best player you can be.

"I just concentrated harder at the plate. I faced that same pitcher many times after that, but only once did he ever strike me out again."

Don went on to win the batting title that year—and to amaze his family and friends with this three-homer game.

MARK LANGSTON

Mark Langston was 14 years old when he faced his first big challenge in baseball. He had to try out for the high school freshman team even though he had a broken toe.

"I didn't think I would make the team," admitted the California Angels' All-Star pitcher. "I was worried because I couldn't run very well. I had to wear an orthopedic shoe that had a hard metal bottom and a plastic top to protect my toe." Despite stiff competition at Buchser High School in his hometown of Santa Clara, California, Mark was equal to the task. Suffering from pain and a bad limp, he gave it his best shot.

Mark had broken his big toe when a wheelbarrow fell on it while he was doing yard work for a neighbor. He had to wear the protective footgear for several weeks because his toe was too swollen to fit into a regular baseball shoe. Although his injury bothered him, he wasn't about to give up sports and wait until his toe healed. He continued to play soccer and sandlot baseball with his friends.

By the time of the high school tryouts, Mark's orthopedic shoe was pretty well beaten up—and he was still hobbling. "I was limping pretty badly," Mark recalled. "I didn't think I had a chance of making the team with the orthopedic shoe on my foot."

Mark had lost some of his confidence. For the first time in his life, he was afraid of failing. He felt his foot hindered him too much.

Then his mom, Ginger, gave him some words of encouragement. "All you can do is go out and try," she told Mark. "If you don't make it, there's always next year. You have nothing to be ashamed of as long as you try."

Mark went to the tryout with renewed confidence. Despite his cast, he ran as hard as he could, nearly hit the cover off the ball, and cleanly fielded everything hit his way. He made such a favorable impression with the coaches that he made the team.

"It was very difficult," Mark said. "But I remembered my mom's advice and gave it everything I had."

Mark worked so hard during the tryout that his orthopedic shoe was destroyed. He had to cut the remnants of the shoe off his foot. A week later, the swelling in his foot had gone down, and he was able to go to baseball practice in a regular shoe.

Mark had never had any problem making a baseball team before. When he was only 5 years old, Mark was such a good player that the older neighborhood boys used to knock on his door and ask him to play. "I had to tell them that Mark was only 5," recalled his mother. "They couldn't believe it. He was as good a ballplayer as any of them."

When Mark was 8 and finally old enough to play in an organized league, he easily made the Key-Rexall team and surprised his family by announcing that he was a pitcher. Until then, no one knew Mark could pitch—or that he even wanted to pitch.

"Mark always wanted to be a catcher even though he was left-handed," his mom said. "We had bought him all the catching gear, including a left-handed catcher's mitt. He used it constantly with his friends in the neighborhood; but the coach wouldn't let him catch on the team. Mark even wore his catching outfit on Halloween when he was trick-or-treating."

The coach did allow Mark to play second base, though, despite the fact that he was left-handed. But Mark continued to improve as a pitcher and became the team's top hurler. Any thoughts of him catching had dimmed until one day when the coach asked for a volunteer to catch. "So I did," Mark recalled. "I told him I had all the gear and even the glove." Mark began to catch in games in which he didn't pitch. And he became such a good catcher that he made the all-star team as both a pitcher and a catcher. "I loved catching," Mark said. "I loved all the gear, and I loved being in on every play."

But when Mark was 13, it was obvious that he was an exceptional pitcher with unlimited potential. So the coach refused to let him catch anymore for fear that Mark might get hurt behind the plate. From then on, Mark concentrated on pitching . . . and winning.

BOB OJEDA

Pitcher

New York Mets

★ ★ ★

Bob Ojeda loved baseball so much that he used to sleep with his uniform on!

The future New York Mets' hurler grew up in Anaheim, about a mile away from the stadium in which the California Angels play baseball. He started learning how to play baseball at the tender age of 2. "Bobby wanted to play all of the time," his dad, Bob, said. "He'd be waiting for me with a mitt, ball, and bat when I came home from work."

When Bob was 5 years old, he wanted to be a baseball player so badly that he made up his own uniform. He donned a cap, old shirt and pants, baseball stirrups, and socks—and wore the entire outfit to bed every night.

Finally, when Bob was 8, he got a new uniform when he joined his first organized team. "Bobby was so proud of it that he switched from wearing the homemade uniform to wearing his new team uniform to bed," said his father.

Bob, whose first Little League team was the Redlegs, said he just couldn't part with his uniform at night. "Not only did I sleep in my uniform, I put my cleats at the end of the bed so I could get into them right away when I woke up in the morning."

Bob couldn't get enough baseball. He even played ball in the house with his dad. The two of them used to drive his mom, Dora, crazy. The living room, family room, hallways, and dining room were all indoor baseball diamonds. "I'd pitch a plastic ball to Bob, and he'd hit it with a plastic bat," his dad said. "The ball would go all over the house. Dora tried to get us to stop, but we never would."

Father and son also played "Burn-Out" with a rubber ball in the backyard, trying to see who could throw the hardest. "We'd throw a plastic baseball around inside when it rained," his dad said. "We would play catch while watching TV. Bobby always had a ball in his hand."

Bob played first base until he was 12 years old because his father didn't let him pitch until then. "Coaches would get angry at me for refusing to let Bobby pitch," his dad said. "But I didn't care. I was protecting Bobby's arm."

When he finally gave Bob permission to pitch, his dad insisted on some strict rules. Bob could only pitch one game a week and could not throw curve balls. "I refused to have the coaches pitch Bobby too much," his dad said. "I'd even lie to them so they wouldn't pitch him. I'd tell them Bobby had a sore arm and he couldn't pitch."

When Bob pitched in high school, his coaches demanded that he throw curves like the other boys. But his father told the coaches in no uncertain terms that Bob wasn't going to throw curves. "Bobby was very fast," his dad said. "He didn't need to throw curves to get batters out at that age. Yet his coaches would get angry with me because I refused to allow him to throw curves. I had spoken with many orthopedic surgeons about the curve ball. They all told me that they were treating boys who injured their arms by throwing curves."

Although the coaches didn't like it, Bob never threw a curve ball until after he left high school. "Don't throw curve balls," Bob tells kids today. "You don't need them at the high school level. If you do throw curves, you'll only hurt your arm." By following his dad's advice, Bob developed a strong arm that eventually got him to the major leagues.

In order to publish this book for the start of the 1991 baseball season, it was necessary to finish it by the end of the 1990 season. As a result, it does not reflect any change of teams that a player might have made since the completion of the manuscript.

Throughout this book, we use the name Little League when we are referring specifically to teams that play official Little League Baseball. We use the term little league — without the capital letters — when we are referring to any other youth-oriented organized baseball.

Will Clark

little BIG LEAGUERS™

Kevin Seitzer

little BIG LEAGUERS™

Darryl Strawberry

little BIG LEAGUERS™

Gregg Olson

little BIG LEAGUERS™

Andre Dawson
little BIG LEAGUERS™

Kirby Puckett

little BIG LEAGUERS™

Barry Larkin

little BIG LEAGUERS™

Nick Esasky

little BIG LEAGUERS™

Jim Abbott

little BIG LEAGUERS™

★ Darryl Strawberry ★

Outfielder • New York Mets

Born: March 12, 1962, Los Angeles, CA
Height: 6'6" Weight: 200 lbs
Bats: L Throws: L

———————

Darryl loved his baseball cap so much that he wore it from the time he got up in the morning until he went to sleep at night. And sometimes he even wore it to bed.

Darryl, the National League Rookie of the Year in 1983, is the Mets' all-time leader in homers, extra-base hits, and RBI. The seven-time All-Star belted 39 homers in both 1987 and 1988.

little BIG LEAGUERS™

★ Kevin Seitzer ★

Third Baseman
Kansas City Royals

Born: March 26, 1962, Springfield, IL
Height: 5'11" Weight: 180 lbs
Bats: R Throws: R

———————

Once when Kevin was 9 years old, he hit what appeared to be a game-tying, last-inning home run. But he made such a wide turn rounding third base that he ran into one of his own teammates. By the time Kevin got untangled, he was tagged out at the plate to end the game.

Kevin became the first Royal to hit over .300 in his first two years in the majors. A two-time All-Star, Kevin led the league in hits in 1987 with 207.

little BIG LEAGUERS™

★ Will Clark ★

First Baseman
San Francisco Giants

Born: March 13, 1964, New Orleans, LA
Height: 6'1" Weight: 190 lbs
Bats: L Throws: L

———————

If it hadn't been for Flash, the family dog, Will might never have become a first baseman. When Will was 2½, his dog came home with a left-handed first baseman's glove in his mouth. Two weeks later, Flash trotted home with a nearly identical mitt. Will used those gloves throughout his childhood.

In 1989, the three-time All-Star was among the top five in batting average (.333), RBI (111), multi-hit games (53), runs scored (104), hits (196), and doubles (38).

little BIG LEAGUERS™

★ Kirby Puckett ★

Outfielder • Minnesota Twins

Born: March 14, 1961, Chicago, IL
Height: 5'8" Weight: 213 lbs
Bats: R Throws: R

———————

Kirby learned to play baseball in a concrete canyon—a housing project on Chicago's South Side with wall-to-wall, sixteen-story buildings. Kirby and his pals painted squares on the sides of the buildings to mark the bases.

Kirby, a five-time All-Star, has hit over .300 every year since 1986, including a whopping .356 in 1988. He also has won four straight Gold Gloves.

little BIG LEAGUERS™

★ Andre Dawson ★

Outfielder • Chicago Cubs

Born: July 10, 1954, Miami, FL
Height: 6'3" Weight: 195 lbs
Bats: R Throws: R

———————

Once when Andre was 9 years old, he was scratched from the lineup after he protested the coach's choice of players for the starting team.

In 1987, Andre swatted 49 homers and drove in 137 runs to earn the National League's Most Valuable Player award. An eight-time Gold Glove winner, Andre played in his seventh straight All-Star game in 1990.

little BIG LEAGUERS™

★ Gregg Olson ★

Pitcher • Baltimore Orioles

Born: October 11, 1966, Omaha, NE
Height: 6'4" Weight: 210 lbs
Bats: R Throws: R

———————

Pitching for a Little League championship, Gregg lost his control, so the opposing coach ordered his batters not to swing at any of Gregg's pitches. Gregg walked six straight batters before his dad scolded the coach for poor sportsmanship. The coach then let his batters swing away.

In 1989, Gregg was named the American League's Rookie of the Year after setting a record for the most saves by a rookie (27).

little BIG LEAGUERS™

★ Jim Abbott ★

Pitcher • California Angels

Born: September 19, 1967, Flint, MI
Height: 6'3" Weight: 200 lbs
Bats: L Throws: L

———————

Nothing was going to stop Jim from playing baseball—not even the fact that he was born with a deformed right hand. Although people doubted him, young Jim learned how to bat, field, and even pitch despite his birth defect.

Jim pitched the United States to an Olympic gold medal when he defeated Japan 5-3 in 1988. The next year, he joined the Angels, posting a 12-12 record with a 3.92 ERA. He struck out 115 batters and tossed 2 shutouts.

little BIG LEAGUERS™

★ Nick Esasky ★

First Baseman
Atlanta Braves

Born: February 24, 1960, Hialeah, FL
Height: 6'3" Weight: 200 lbs
Bats: R Throws: R

———————

Teaching Nick how to hit and field turned into a family affair. Almost every night, Nick, his parents, four sisters, and a younger brother went to a nearby park, where Nick took batting and fielding practice.

Nick enjoyed a career year in 1989 when, with the Boston Red Sox, he walloped 30 homers and drove in 108 runs.

little BIG LEAGUERS™

★ Barry Larkin ★

Shortstop • Cincinnati Reds

Born: April 28, 1964, Cincinnati, OH
Height: 6'0" Weight: 185 lbs
Bats: R Throws: R

———————

Although he had a great arm, Barry hated to pitch. Once, when he was 13, he deliberately stalled on the mound, taking a couple of minutes between pitches, until the umpire threw him out of the game.

A three-time All-Star, Barry was the top offensive shortstop in 1989 with a batting average of .342.

little BIG LEAGUERS™

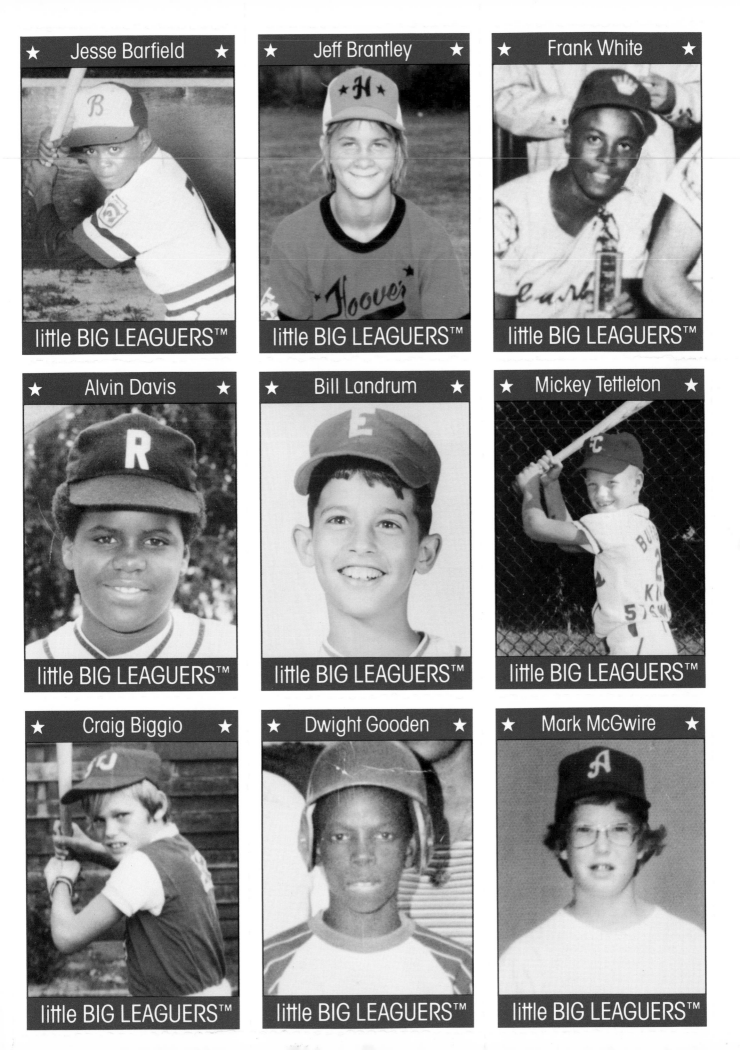

★ Frank White ★

Second Baseman
Kansas City Royals

Born: September 4, 1950, Greenville, MS
Height: 5'11" Weight: 190 lbs
Bats: R Throws: R

Frank thought that catcher was the easiest position to play—until he tried it. After the first pitch hit him in the head and the next two hit him on the knees, he walked off the field and never caught again.

Frank has won more Gold Gloves than any other second baseman—eight. A five-time All-Star, Frank was named the MVP of the 1980 American League Championship Series. He has collected more than 2,000 career hits.

little BIG LEAGUERS™

★ Jeff Brantley ★

Pitcher
San Francisco Giants

Born: September 5, 1963, Florence, AL
Height: 5'11" Weight: 180 lbs
Bats: R Throws: R

When Jeff started playing third base for his Little League team, he couldn't throw the ball across the infield on the fly because his arm was too weak. So for hours at a time, he threw a rubber ball against the house and caught it. Over time, his arm became so strong, he became a pitcher.

In 1989, his first full season in the majors, Jeff was 7-0 in relief and ranked third among the league's most effective rookie relievers.

little BIG LEAGUERS™

★ Jesse Barfield ★

Outfielder • New York Yankees

Born: October 29, 1959, Joliet, IL
Height: 6'1" Weight: 200 lbs
Bats: R Throws: R

As a little league pitcher, Jesse would get so upset when he lost a game that he wouldn't eat for two or three days. Finally, his mother told him that he couldn't pitch anymore unless he learned to live with defeat.

In 1989, Jesse, a two-time Gold Glove winner, led American League outfielders by gunning down 20 base runners. The All-Star belted 40 homers in 1986, tops in the league.

little BIG LEAGUERS™

★ Mickey Tettleton ★

Catcher • Baltimore Orioles

Born: September 16, 1960, Oklahoma City, OK
Height: 6'2" Weight: 212 lbs
Bats: Both Throws: R

Mickey sharpened his batting stroke as a kid by hitting baseballs that he made out of newspapers and electrical tape. He would throw the ball onto the roof of his house and then hit it as it fell off.

Mickey made the All-Star team in his first year as a starter in 1989. That year, he walloped 26 home runs and won the American League Silver Slugger award for catchers.

little BIG LEAGUERS™

★ Bill Landrum ★

Pitcher • Pittsburgh Pirates

Born: August 17, 1958, Columbia, SC
Height: 6'2" Weight: 205 lbs
Bats: R Throws: R

Bill used to get so mad if an umpire's call went against him that he would walk off the mound and refuse to pitch. Finally, his mother told Bill that if he didn't stop it, he couldn't play anymore. He stopped it.

As the Pirates' most effective relief pitcher in 1989, Bill led the team in appearances (56) and saves (26). His sparkling 1.67 ERA was the fourth best among the league's relievers.

little BIG LEAGUERS™

★ Alvin Davis ★

First Baseman
Seattle Mariners

Born: September 9, 1960, Riverside, CA
Height: 6'1" Weight: 190 lbs
Bats: L Throws: R

Alvin learned how to hit by playing whiffle ball with his two older brothers, and by using an old real estate sign behind home plate to determine the strike zone.

Alvin, the American League's Rookie of the Year in 1984, enjoyed a career-high .305 batting average in 1989, leading the Mariners with 95 RBI and 30 doubles.

little BIG LEAGUERS™

★ Mark McGwire ★

First Baseman
Oakland Athletics

Born: October 1, 1963, Pomona, CA
Height: 6'5" Weight: 225 lbs
Bats: R Throws: R

Mark was destined to be a star for the Oakland Athletics. When he was 10 years old, Mark joined a Little League team called the Athletics and was a slugger and a leader, just like he is now. Even the uniform was the same as he wears now—gold, green, and white.

In 1987, after pounding 49 homers and driving in 118 RBI, Mark was named the American League's Rookie of the Year. Since he broke into the majors, Mark has appeared in four straight All-Star games and three World Series.

little BIG LEAGUERS™

★ Dwight Gooden ★

Pitcher • New York Mets

Born: November 16, 1964, Tampa, FL
Height: 6'3" Weight: 210 lbs
Bats: R Throws: R

Dwight felt so uncomfortable playing in front of his parents that once, when he was 8 years old, he walked off the field in the middle of the game when he spotted them in the stands. He was afraid he'd embarrass himself in front of them.

Dwight, the National League's Rookie of the Year in 1984, was the youngest pitcher ever to win the Cy Young award. He won it in 1985 at the age of 20. Known as "Dr. K," Dwight has struck out at least 10 batters in a game more than 40 times.

little BIG LEAGUERS™

★ Craig Biggio ★

Catcher • Houston Astros

Born: December 14, 1965, Smithtown, NY
Height: 5'11" Weight: 180 lbs
Bats: R Throws: R

When Craig was a teenager, he witnessed a heart-wrenching tragedy on the baseball field—a lightning bolt struck and killed his teammate and knocked Craig off his feet just a few yards away.

In 1989, Craig led the major leagues in stolen bases by a catcher with 21, and won the Silver Slugger award for best offensive catcher by clubbing 13 home runs.

little BIG LEAGUERS™

★ John Kruk ★	★ Vince Coleman ★	★ Kevin Mitchell ★
little BIG LEAGUERS™	little BIG LEAGUERS™	little BIG LEAGUERS™
★ Lonnie Smith ★	★ Bobby Thigpen ★	★ Bill Doran ★
little BIG LEAGUERS™	little BIG LEAGUERS™	little BIG LEAGUERS™
★ David Cone ★	★ Kelly Gruber ★	★ Don Slaught ★
little BIG LEAGUERS™	little BIG LEAGUERS™	little BIG LEAGUERS™

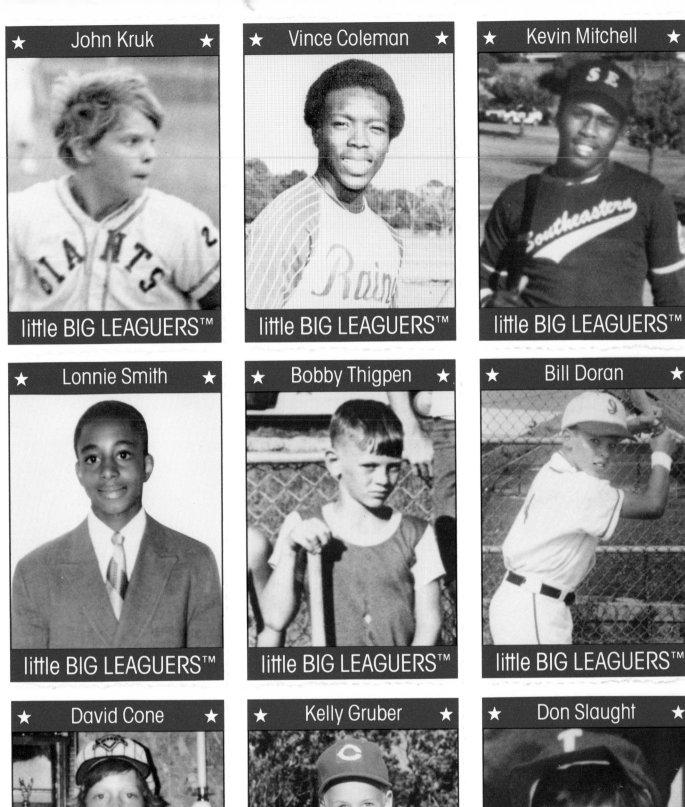

Kevin Mitchell

Outfielder
San Francisco Giants

Born: January 13, 1962, San Diego, CA
Height: 5'11" Weight: 210 lbs
Bats: R Throws: R

As a Little Leaguer, Kevin loved to catch so much that he went to drastic lengths to avoid playing other positions. Once, after the coach ordered him to play left field, a pouting Kevin deliberately dropped an easy fly ball in protest. His error lost the game for his team.

Kevin was named the National League's Most Valuable Player in 1989 when he clubbed 47 homers, drove in 125 runs, and hit .291. That same year, the two-time All-Star homered off every team in the league.

little BIG LEAGUERS™

Vince Coleman

Outfielder
St. Louis Cardinals

Born: September 21, 1961, Jacksonville, FL
Height: 6'0" Weight: 170 lbs
Bats: Both Throws: R

Vince hit the only grand slam of his life when he was in the tenth grade—and it beat his former teammates, who didn't think he was good enough to play with them.

Vince became the first player in major league history to steal 100 or more bases in his first two years. He set another major league mark by swiping 50 consecutive bases without being caught in 1989.

little BIG LEAGUERS™

John Kruk

Outfielder
Philadelphia Phillies

Born: February 9, 1961, Charleston, WV
Height: 5'10" Weight: 194 lbs
Bats: L Throws: L

John grew up in a small town, where sandlot teams had only four players. Since all but John batted right-handed, the kids made a rule that balls hit to right field were outs. So John, a left-handed pull hitter, had no choice but to learn how to hit to the opposite field.

John has hit over .300 in three of his four years in the majors. In 1987, as a San Diego Padre, he hit 20 homers while batting .313.

little BIG LEAGUERS™

Bill Doran

Second Baseman
Cincinnati Reds

Born: May 28, 1958, Cincinnati, OH
Height: 6'0" Weight: 175 lbs
Bats: Both Throws: R

For two years in a row, Bill was one strike away from pitching his Little League team to a local championship. Incredibly, both times he gave up a disastrous game-winning home run—to the same batter!

Named the Astros' Most Valuable Player in 1985 and 1987, Bill led the league in fielding percentage among second basemen in 1987 and 1988.

little BIG LEAGUERS™

Bobby Thigpen

Pitcher • Chicago White Sox

Born: July 17, 1963, Tallahassee, FL
Height: 6'3" Weight: 195 lbs
Bats: R Throws: R

Even though his leg was in a cast from an accident, Bobby still played baseball—on crutches. During a sandlot game, Bobby leaned the crutches against his body and belted out several hits. As soon as he hit, he grabbed his crutches and hobbled around the bases.

In 1988, the All-Star relief pitcher established a White Sox record with 34 saves, and then tied his own mark the following year. In 1990, Bobby set the major league record in saves, with 57.

little BIG LEAGUERS™

Lonnie Smith

Outfielder • Atlanta Braves

Born: December 22, 1955, Chicago, IL
Height: 5'9" Weight: 190 lbs
Bats: R Throws: R

Lonnie was so furious over an umpire's call during a Little League game that he stripped off his uniform in the middle of the field in protest. Then he angrily stormed off the diamond dressed only in his underwear, socks, and baseball shoes.

Lonnie, a veteran of three World Series and an All-Star game, won the National League's Comeback Player of the Year award in 1989 when he hit .315 with 21 homers.

little BIG LEAGUERS™

Don Slaught

Catcher • Pittsburgh Pirates

Born: September 11, 1958, Long Beach, CA
Height: 6'1" Weight: 190 lbs
Bats: R Throws: R

In his first Little League game as a catcher, Don crouched too hard and too fast—and split his pants. As soon as the inning was over, he raced across the street to his home, changed his pants, and returned to the game.

In 1989, Don threw out 26 runners attempting to steal and posted a fine .991 fielding percentage. That same year, he also batted .304 with runners in scoring position.

little BIG LEAGUERS™

Kelly Gruber

Third Baseman
Toronto Blue Jays

Born: February 26, 1962, Bellaire, TX
Height: 6'0" Weight: 185 lbs
Bats: R Throws: R

Kelly dedicated all his games to his grandparents. They were his inspiration. He'd call out their names and wave to them from the field during games.

Kelly, whose first major league hit was a pinch-hit home run against the Boston Red Sox, hit .290 with 18 homers in 1989 and was named to the All-Star team in 1990.

little BIG LEAGUERS™

David Cone

Pitcher • New York Mets

Born: January 2, 1963, Kansas City, MO
Height: 6'1" Weight: 190 lbs
Bats: L Throws: R

In a Little League game, David made a wild throw that hit the umpire smack in the head and momentarily knocked him out. David was so scared that the umpire would beat him up, he ran into the dugout and refused to come out.

In 1988, the Mets' All-Star recorded a stunning 20-3 record—the sixth-best winning percentage (.870) in baseball history for 20-game winners.

little BIG LEAGUERS™

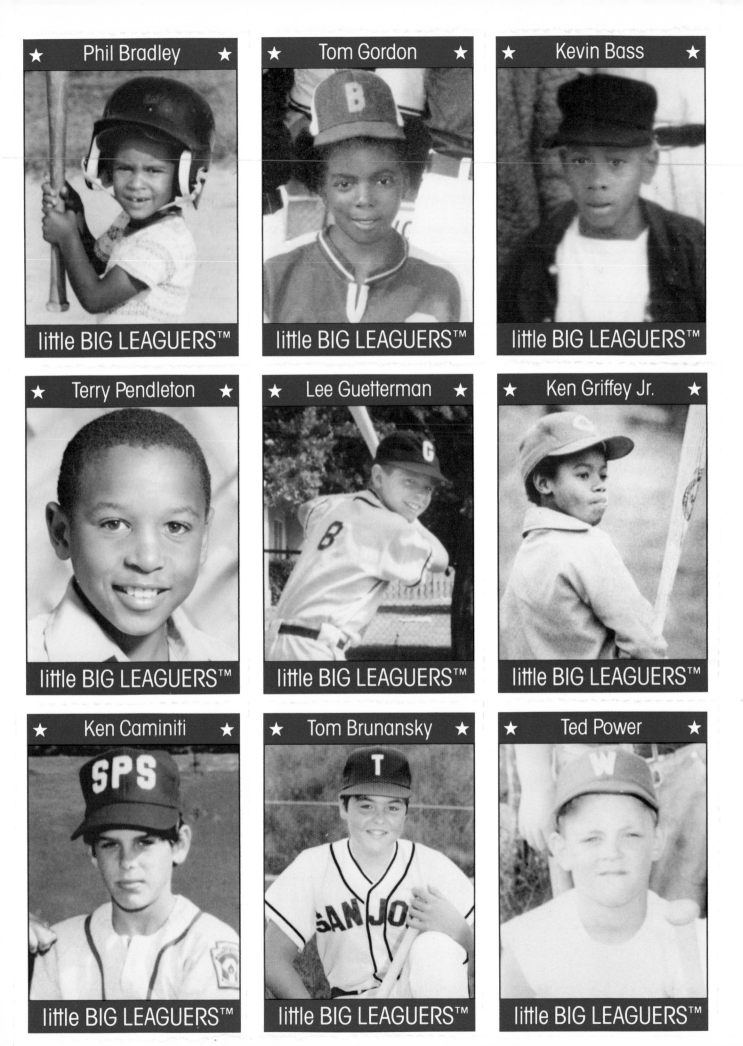

Kevin Bass

Outfielder
San Francisco Giants

Born: May 12, 1959, Redwood City, CA
Height: 6'0"   Weight: 180 lbs
Bats: Both   Throws: R

The first time Kevin tried switching-hitting in Little League, he went 7 for 7 and wore out the opposition's entire pitching staff. But despite his phenomenal success, Kevin refused to switch-hit again until he was in high school.

In 1987, Kevin became the first National Leaguer to homer from both sides of the plate in the same game twice in the same season.

little BIG LEAGUERS™

Tom Gordon

Pitcher • Kansas City Royals

Born: November 18, 1967, Sebring, FL
Height: 5'9"   Weight: 160 lbs
Bats: R   Throws: R

Tom was such a phenomenal pitcher that he started playing against adults when he was only 13 years old—for pay!

Tom wowed the American League in his rookie year of 1989 when he posted a remarkable 17-9 record and a 3.64 ERA. He finished second in the league in strikeouts per nine innings with 8.4 and was named the league's Rookie Pitcher of the Year by *The Sporting News.*

little BIG LEAGUERS™

Phil Bradley

Outfielder
Chicago White Sox

Born: March 11, 1959, Bloomington, IN
Height: 6'0"   Weight: 190 lbs
Bats: R   Throws: R

Phil learned a lot about baseball in college—beginning when he was 10 years old. His dad was coach of the Virginia State University baseball team and let Phil act as the warm-up catcher for pitchers during practice.

In 1989, the All-Star outfielder became the first Baltimore Oriole to finish the season with at least 10 doubles, 10 triples, 10 homers, and 10 stolen bases. He also led the Orioles in runs scored with 83.

little BIG LEAGUERS™

Ken Griffey Jr.

Outfielder • Seattle Mariners

Born: November 21, 1969, Donora, PA
Height: 6'3"   Weight: 195 lbs
Bats: L   Throws: L

Ken was sucn an outstanding player in his first year in Little League that he never made an out as a batter and never lost a game as a pitcher. But when he made an out in his first at-bat the following year, he broke down and cried.

Ken, who began playing in the majors in 1989 when he was just 19 years old, swatted 16 homers and batted .264. He was the American League's starting center fielder in the 1990 All-Star Game.

little BIG LEAGUERS™

Lee Guetterman

Pitcher • New York Yankees

Born: November 22, 1958, Chattanooga, TN
Height: 6'8"   Weight: 227 lbs
Bats: L   Throws: L

Before pitching in a big all-star game when he was 12 years old, Lee was told by his coach to rub heating balm on his arm. Lee did. Unfortunately, his arm went numb and Lee was clobbered in the game.

Lee was the most consistent Yankee relief pitcher in 1989 with 13 saves and a 2.45 ERA. He holds the major league record of 30.2 scoreless innings by a relief pitcher at the start of a season.

little BIG LEAGUERS™

Terry Pendleton

Third Baseman
St. Louis Cardinals

Born: July 16, 1960, Los Angeles, CA
Height: 5'9"   Weight: 195 lbs
Bats: Both   Throws: R

In his first year of Little League, Terry got only one hit and struck out almost every time he came to bat. But he didn't give up. He spent the entire winter learning how to hit. The next season, Terry made the all-star team.

A Gold Glove at third base, Terry led National League third sackers in total chances and assists in 1986 and 1987, and was named the league's best defensive third baseman by *Baseball America.*

little BIG LEAGUERS™

Ted Power

Pitcher • Pittsburgh Pirates

Born: January 31, 1955, Guthrie, OK
Height: 6'4"   Weight: 220 lbs
Bats: R   Throws: R

When Ted was 7 years old, he had great control as a pitcher. But once, when he had to pee really badly, he walked six batters in an inning. Finally, the coach called time. Ted ran a block away and relieved himself behind a tree, and then returned to the mound, where he regained his control.

In 1987, Ted led the Cincinnati Reds in games started (34), innings pitched (204), strikeouts (133), and wins (10).

little BIG LEAGUERS™

Tom Brunansky

Outfielder • Boston Red Sox

Born: August 20, 1960, Covina, CA
Height: 6'4"   Weight: 216 lbs
Bats: R   Throws: R

Every time Tom made a big play on the Little League field, he heard the loud, happy honking coming from his father's car parked on a hill above the field. His dad was too excitable to watch Tom's games from the stands.

In 1989, Tom became the only active player in the majors to stroke 50 or more extra-base hits in eight consecutive seasons.

little BIG LEAGUERS™

Ken Caminiti

Third Baseman
Houston Astros

Born: April 21, 1963, Hanford, CA
Height: 6'3"   Weight: 200 lbs
Bats: Both   Throws: R

Ken hated to bat when he was in Little League because he was deathly afraid of being hit with a pitch. He didn't overcome his fear until he reached high school.

In 1989, his first full year in the majors, Ken led the Astros in doubles with 31 and was second in RBI with 71. *Baseball America* named Ken the infielder with the best throwing arm in the National League.

little BIG LEAGUERS™

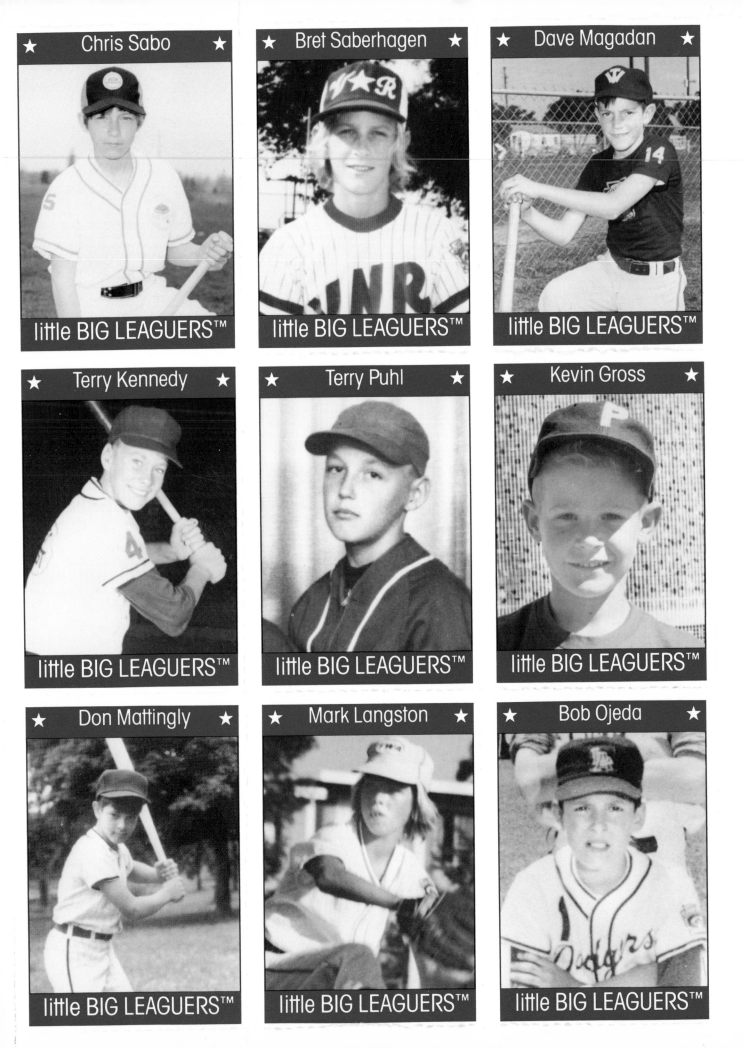

Dave Magadan
★ ★

First Baseman
New York Mets

Born: September 30, 1962, Tampa, FL
Height: 6'3" Weight: 200 lbs
Bats: L Throws: R

___

Dave and his brother, Joe, constantly played ball in their backyard, but they accidentally kept breaking the windows of their house. Dave once shattered a window that his father had fixed only the day before.

One of the Mets' best clutch hitters, Dave batted .300 with players in scoring position and two outs in 1989. The following year, Dave had the second-highest batting average in the league with .328.

little BIG LEAGUERS™

Bret Saberhagen
★ ★

Pitcher • Kansas City Royals

Born: April 11, 1964, Chicago Heights, IL
Height: 6'1" Weight: 195 lbs
Bats: R Throws: R

___

Bret thought he was too good to practice before his first Little League tryout. He was wrong. He muffed pop-ups and couldn't hit the ball out of the infield. He was so bad that he was one of the last players drafted in the league.

The All-Star hurler is only the fourth player in American League history to have won at least two Cy Young awards (in 1985 and 1989). He was the Comeback Player of the Year in 1987 and the MVP of the 1985 World Series.

little BIG LEAGUERS™

Chris Sabo
★ ★

Third Baseman
Cincinnati Reds

Born: January 19, 1962, Detroit, MI
Height: 6'0" Weight: 185 lbs
Bats: R Throws: R

___

When Chris wasn't playing baseball as a teenager, he was umpiring league games. He quickly discovered that being an ump was a lot tougher than he thought. He was the target of so many insults and jeers that he soon quit.

Chris's first year in the majors, 1988, was a dream season. He was the only rookie in either league to play in the All-Star Game and wound up the season by being named the National League's Rookie of the Year.

little BIG LEAGUERS™

Kevin Gross
★ ★

Pitcher • Montreal Expos

Born: June 8, 1961, Downey, CA
Height: 6'5" Weight: 215 lbs
Bats: R Throws: R

___

When Kevin was 12, he was the smallest player on his team. Yet opposing coaches in an all-star tournament tried to ban him from pitching—because he was too good!

Kevin, an All-Star hurler in 1988, has been a dependable starting pitcher. Through 1989, he had pitched at least 200 innings five years in a row, averaging more than 11 wins per season.

little BIG LEAGUERS™

Terry Puhl
★ ★

Outfielder • Houston Astros

Born: July 8, 1956
Melville, Saskatchewan, Canada
Height: 6'2" Weight: 200 lbs
Bats: L Throws: R

___

Growing up on the plains of Saskatchewan, Canada, Terry had to travel great distances to play baseball. His dad would pack Terry and his Little League teammates into an old army bus and drive 100 miles or more to play other teams.

In 1989, Terry handled 207 chances in the outfield without an error, tops in the National League. One of the league's best clutch batters, Terry led his team in pinch hits with 15 in 1987.

little BIG LEAGUERS™

Terry Kennedy
★ ★

Catcher
San Francisco Giants

Born: June 4, 1956, Euclid, OH
Height: 6'4" Weight: 230 lbs
Bats: L Throws: R

___

Terry lived the life other Little Leaguers only dream about. Because his dad, Bob, was a major league manager, Terry hung around with super stars. He played catch with Catfish Hunter, took batting practice with Reggie Jackson, and shagged fly balls with Billy Williams.

Terry, who has played in All-Star games for both leagues, had the second-best fielding percentage (.994) among American League catchers in 1988. He was the majors' top-hitting catcher in 1983 with a .284 batting average.

little BIG LEAGUERS™

Bob Ojeda
★ ★

Pitcher • New York Mets

Born: December 17, 1957, Los Angeles, CA
Height: 6'1" Weight: 195 lbs
Bats: L Throws: L

___

Bob loved baseball so much as a kid that he used to sleep with his uniform on. He went to bed wearing his cap, jersey, pants, stirrups, and socks—with his cleats at the foot of the bed.

Bob enjoyed a career year in 1986 when he led the National League in winning percentage (.783) with a super 18-5 record. He also had the league's second-best ERA, 2.57.

little BIG LEAGUERS™

Mark Langston
★ ★

Pitcher • California Angels

Born: August 20, 1960, San Diego, CA
Height: 6'2" Weight: 190 lbs
Bats: R Throws: L

___

Mark was 14 when he faced his first big challenge in baseball. He had to try out for the high school freshman team even though he had a broken toe. Despite wearing an orthopedic shoe, Mark impressed the coaches and made the team.

In 1988, when Mark was with the Seattle Mariners, the All-Star pitched a club-record 34.1 consecutive scoreless innings and set another team record with 16 strikeouts in a game.

little BIG LEAGUERS™

Don Mattingly
★ ★

First Baseman
New York Yankees

Born: April 20, 1961, Evansville, IN
Height: 6'0" Weight: 192 lbs
Bats: L Throws: L

___

During one memorable game when Don was 10 years old, every time he heard friends yell for him to blast a home run, he belted one—right where they had wanted him to hit it. He swatted three round-trippers—one to each field.

Don became only the sixth Yankee in history—the first in nearly fifty years—to hit .300 or better in six consecutive years. Don has been named to six All-Star games and has earned five consecutive Gold Gloves.

little BIG LEAGUERS™